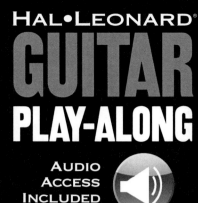

HAL•LEONARD®
GUITAR
PLAY-ALONG

AUDIO
ACCESS
INCLUDED

PLAYBACK+
Speed • Pitch • Balance • Loop

CONTENTS

Cover photo © Eddie Malluk/Atlasicons.com

To access audio, visit:
www.halleonard.com/mylibrary

Enter Code
"4085-0901-6973-2372"

ISBN 978-1-4768-7448-7

HAL•LEONARD®

Visit Hal Leonard Online at
www.halleonard.com

Contact us:
Hal Leonard
7777 West Bluemound Road
Milwaukee, WI 53213
Email: info@halleonard.com

In Europe, contact:
Hal Leonard Europe Limited
42 Wigmore Street
Marylebone, London, W1U 2RN
Email: info@halleonardeurope.com

In Australia, contact:
Hal Leonard Australia Pty. Ltd.
4 Lentara Court
Cheltenham, Victoria, 3192 Australia
Email: info@halleonard.com.au

Best of Both Worlds

Words and Music by Edward Van Halen, Alex Van Halen, Michael Anthony and Sammy Hagar

Intro
Moderately ♩ = 116

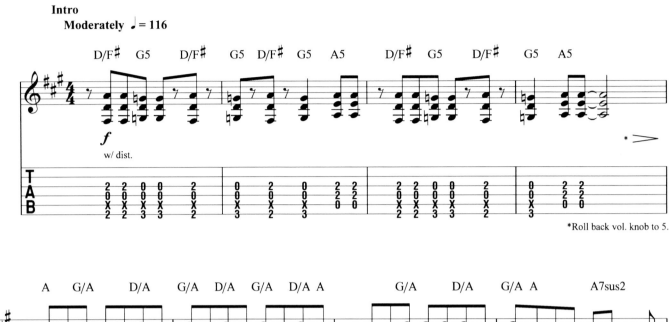

*Roll back vol. knob to 5.

**Swell w/ vol. knob to 10.

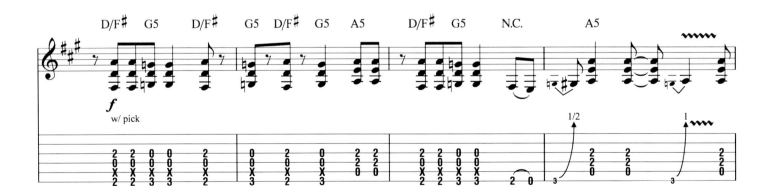

Verse

1. I don't know __ what I've been __ liv-ing on, __ but it's not e-nough to fill me up.

I need more __ than just, a, words can say; __

I need ev-'ry-thing this life can give __ me. Hey, __ hey, __ yeah!

*Bass plays A throughout verses.
**Roll back vol. knob to 5.
***Swell w/ vol. knob to 10.

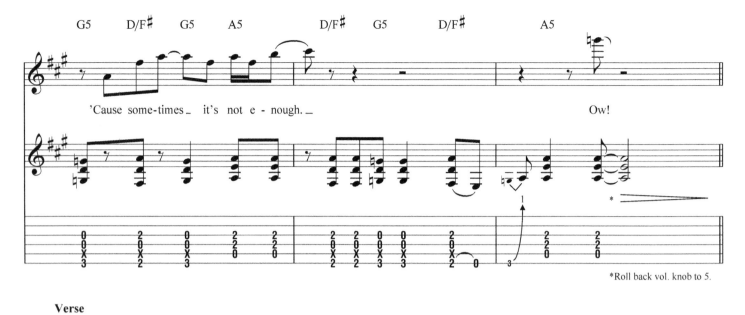

'Cause some-times _ it's not e - nough. _ Ow!

*Roll back vol. knob to 5.

Verse

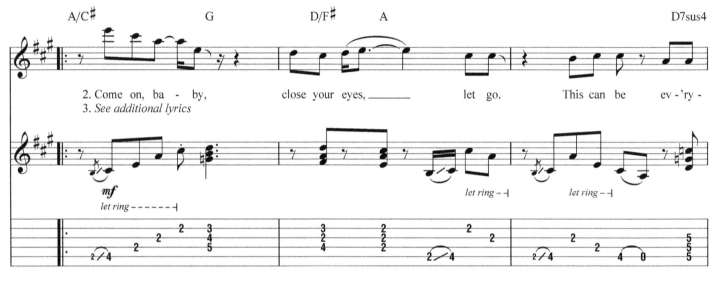

2. Come on, ba - by, close your eyes, _____ let go. This can be ev - 'ry -
3. *See additional lyrics*

mf

let ring

let ring

let ring

2nd time, substitute Fill 1

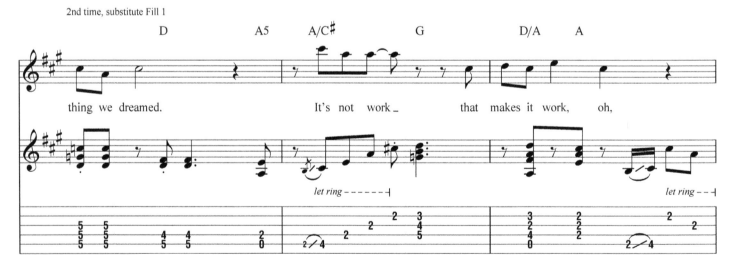

thing we dreamed. It's not work _ that makes it work, oh,

let ring

let ring

Fill 1

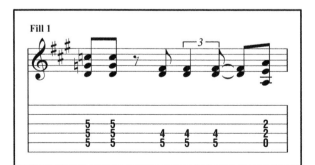

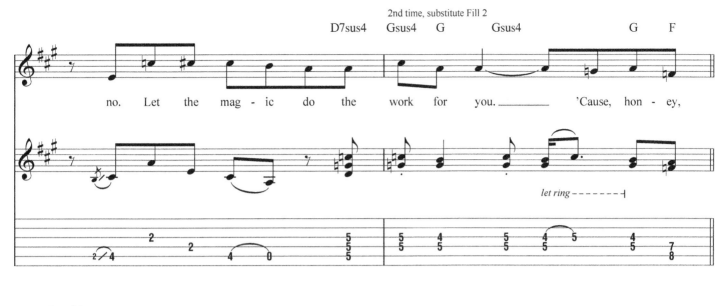

2nd time, substitute Fill 2

D7sus4 Gsus4 G Gsus4 G F

no. Let the mag - ic do the work for you. _____ 'Cause, hon - ey,

let ring - - - - - - - ┤

Pre-Chorus

N.C. Fsus2 C/E Esus4 E Esus4 E

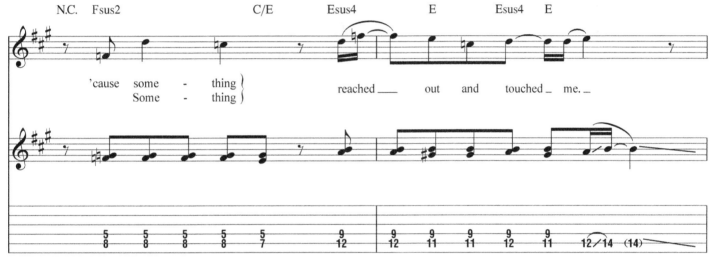

'cause some - thing }
Some - thing }

reached ___ out and touched _ me. _

Bsus4 B Dadd9 Fmaj7

Now I know that all I want, I want the

let ring - - - - - - ┤

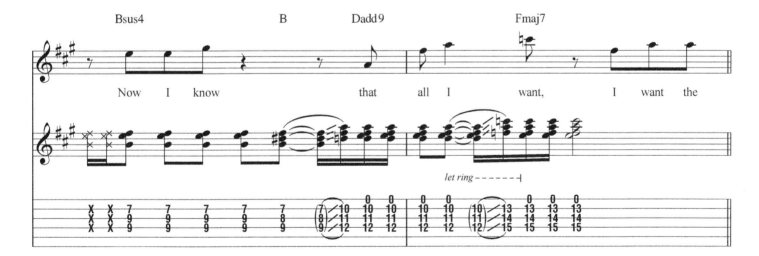

Fill 2

5

Chorus

2nd time, substitute Fill 3

*Set vol. knob to 10.

best of both worlds _ and, hon - ey, I ____ know _ what it's worth.

If we could have the best of both worlds, _ {we'd have / a lit-tle bit of

heav - en right here on earth, _____ ooh! Woo!

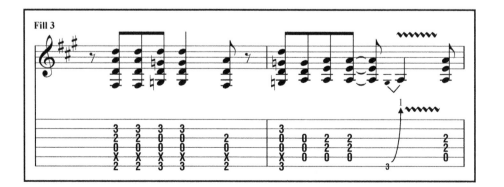

Fill 3

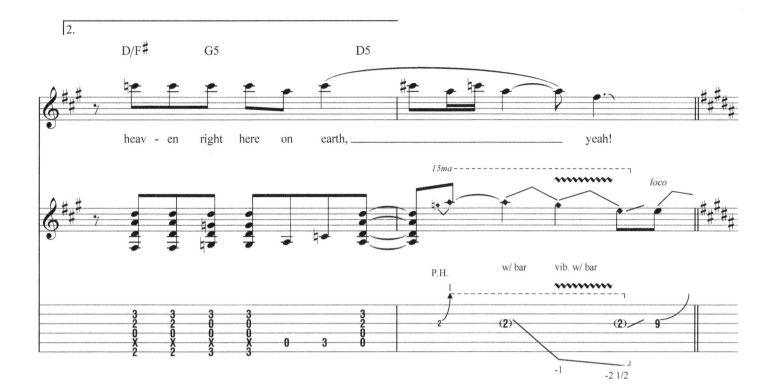

heav - en right here on earth, _____ yeah!

Guitar Solo

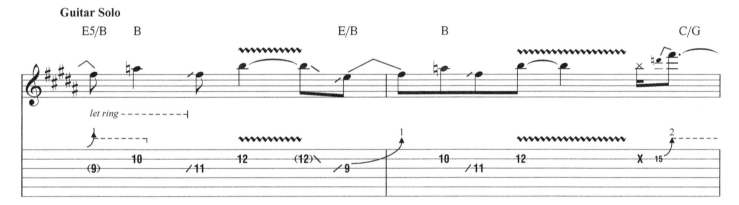

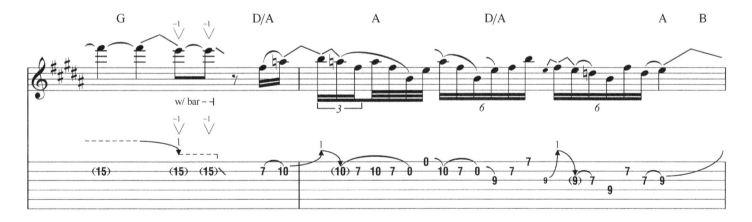

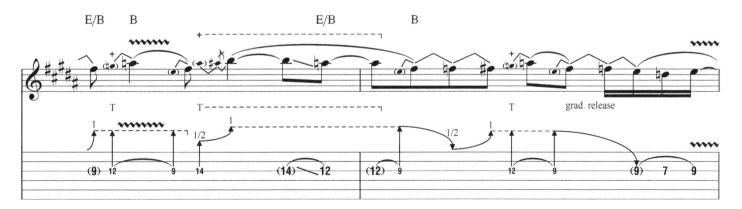

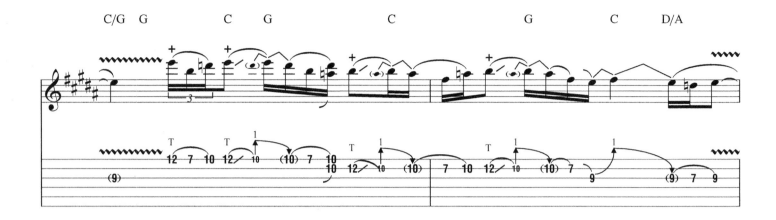

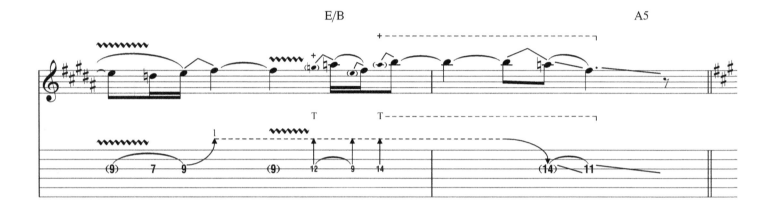

Interlude

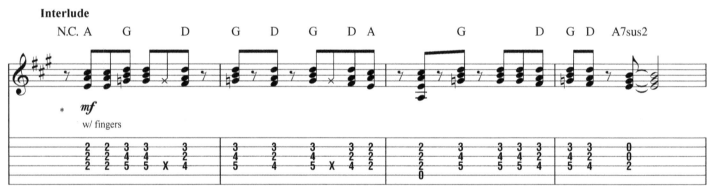

*Roll vol. knob back to 5.

Whoa. _____

Verse

4. Uh, you don't have to die and go to heav - en,____ uh, or hang a - round to be

born a - gain.

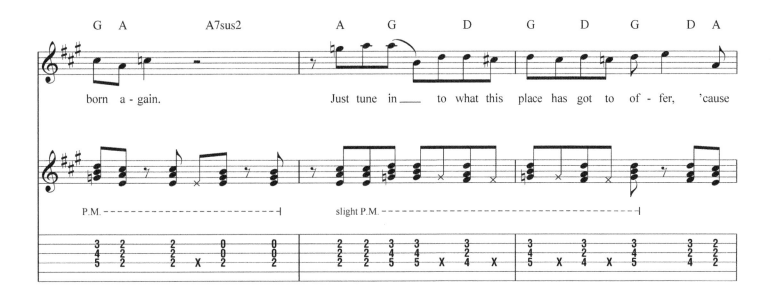

Just tune in ___ to what this place has got to of - fer, 'cause

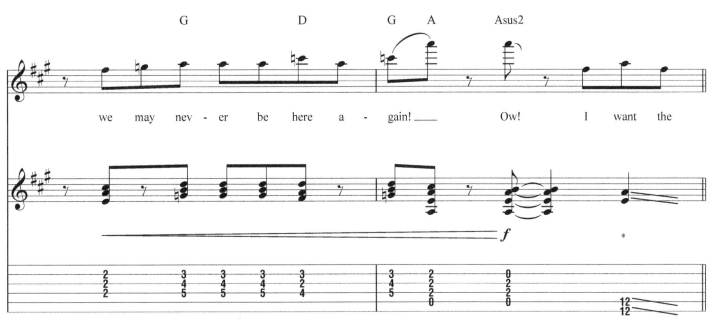

we may nev - er be here a - gain! ___ Ow! I want the

*Roll vol. knob up.

Chorus

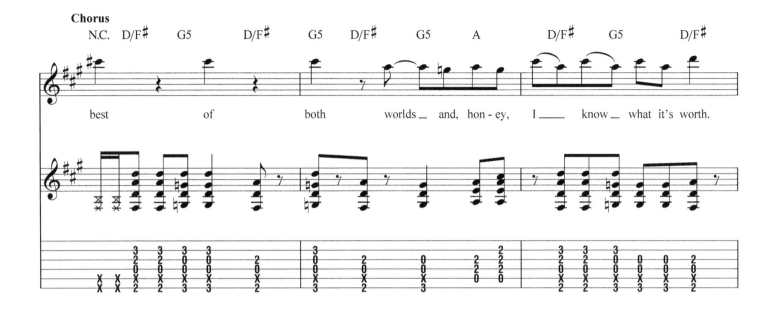

best of both worlds _ and, hon-ey, I _ know _ what it's worth.

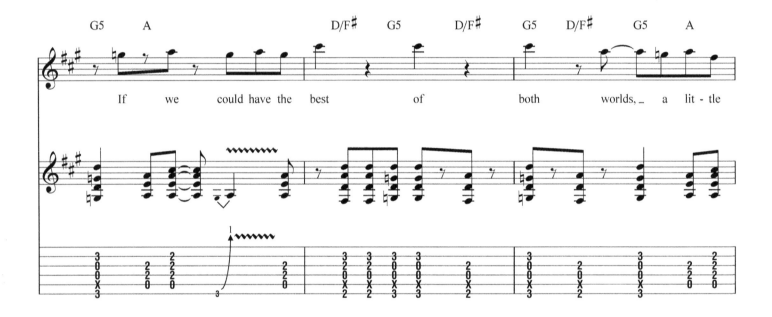

If we could have the best of both worlds, _ a lit-tle

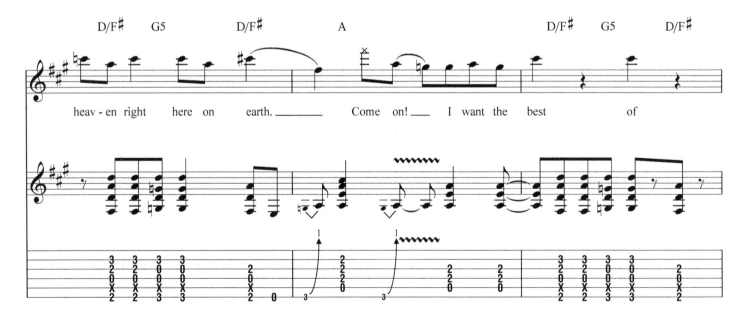

heav-en right here on earth. _____ Come on! _ I want the best of

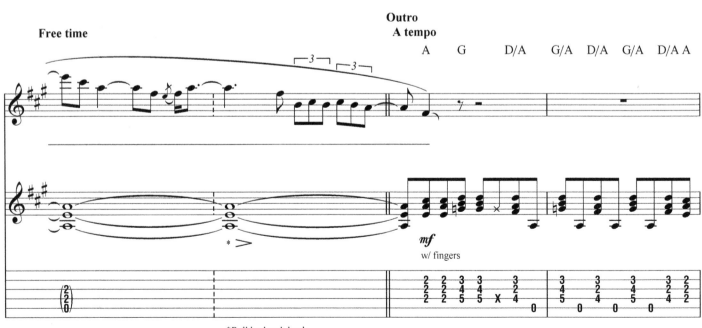

*Roll back vol. knob.

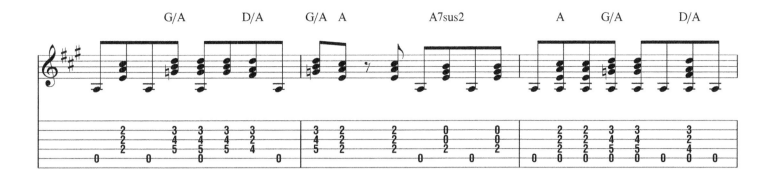

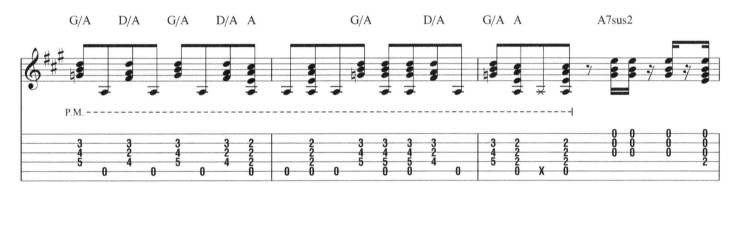

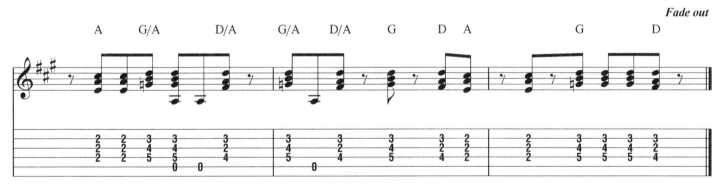

Additional Lyrics

3. Well, there's a picture in a gallery,
   A fallen angel, looks a lot like you.
   We forget where we come from sometimes.
   I had a dream; it was, uh, really you.

Black and Blue

Words and Music by Edward Van Halen, Alex Van Halen, Michael Anthony and Sammy Hagar

Intro
Moderately slow ♩ = 99

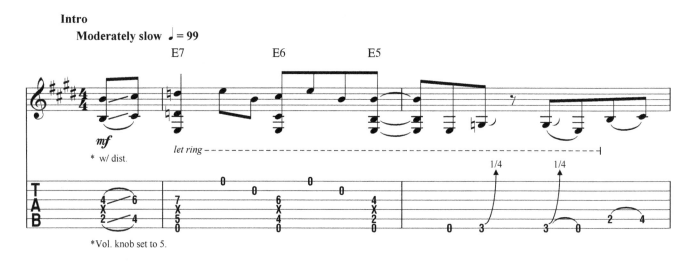

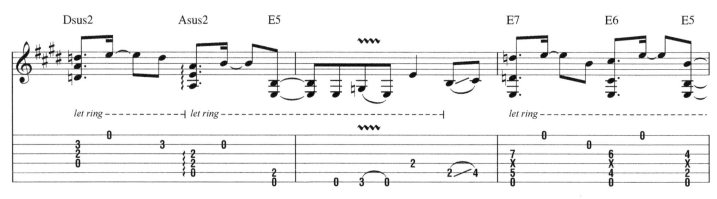

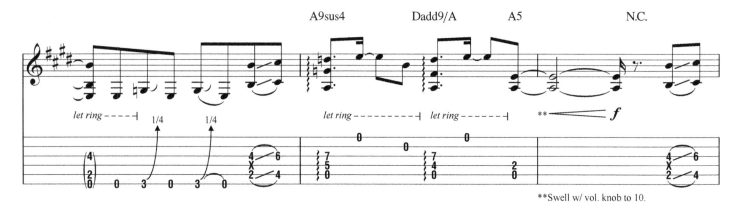

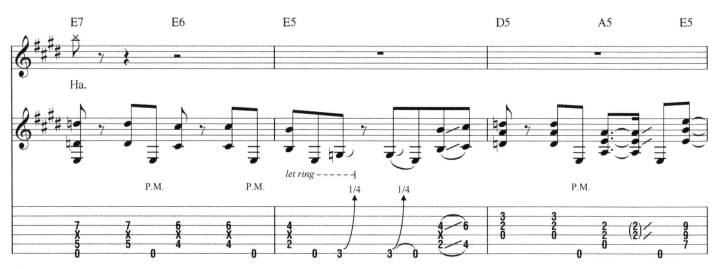

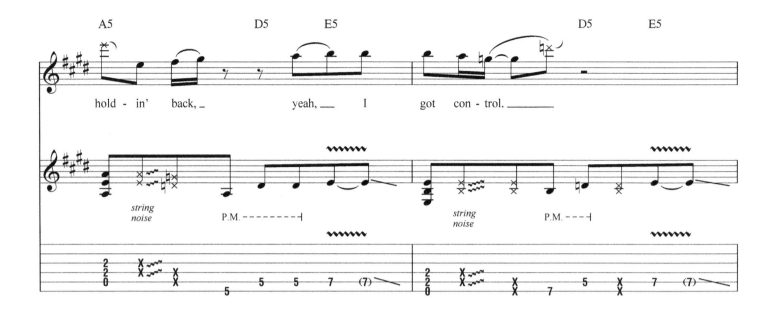

hold - in' back, __ yeah, __ I got con - trol. __

string noise P.M. ———————|

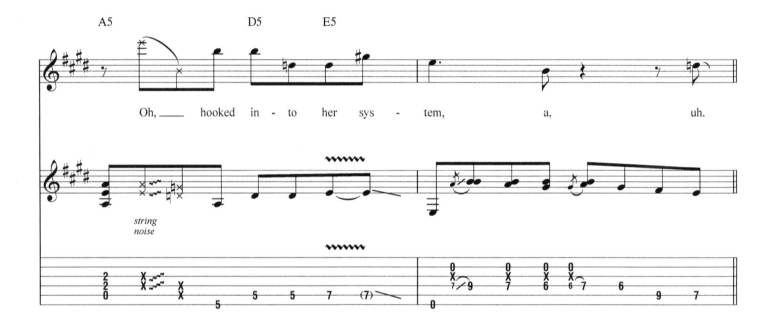

Oh, __ hooked in - to her sys - tem, a, __ uh.

string noise

Chorus

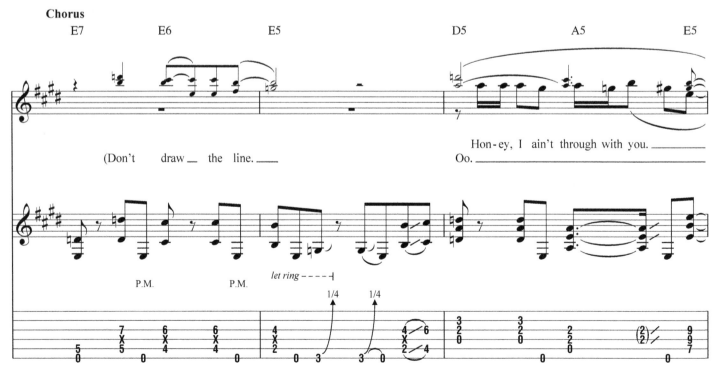

(Don't draw __ the line. __)

Hon - ey, I ain't through with you. __
Oo. __

P.M. P.M. *let ring - - - -|*

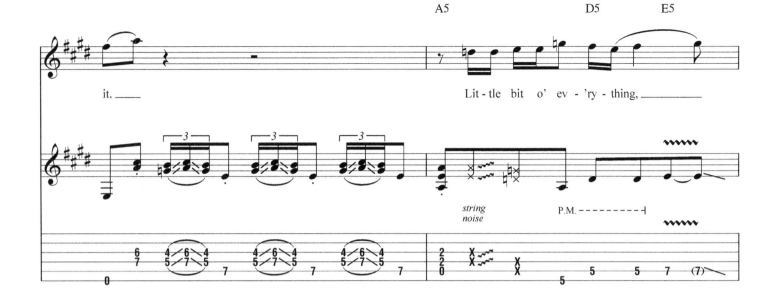

Little bit o' ev-'ry-thing, _____

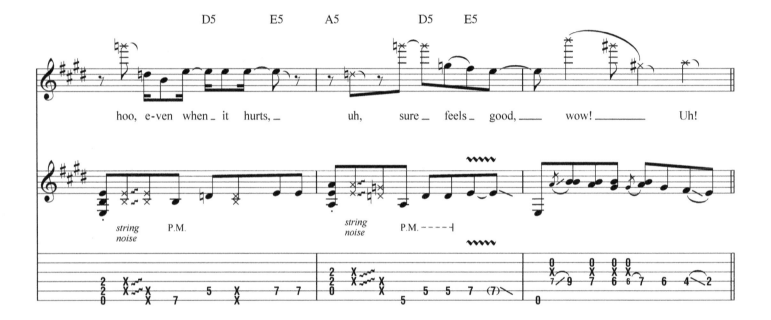

hoo, e-ven when _ it hurts, _ uh, sure _ feels _ good, _____ wow! _____ Uh!

Chorus

(Don't draw _____ the line. _____

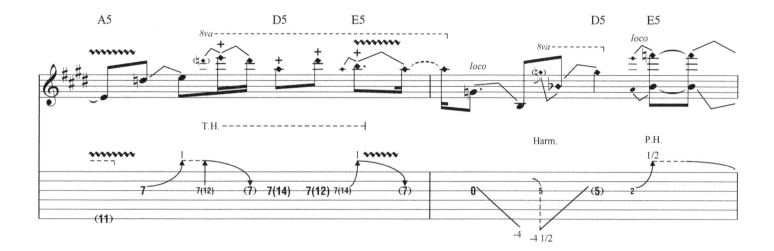

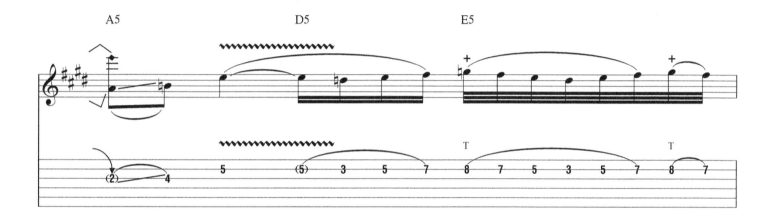

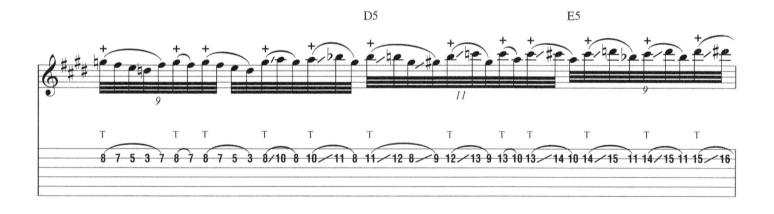

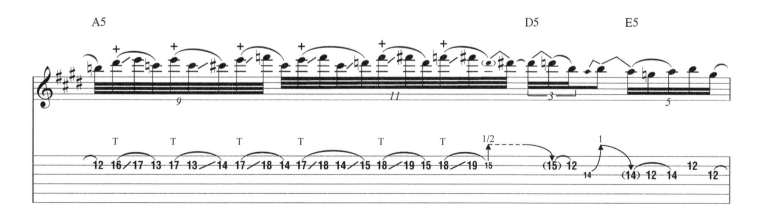

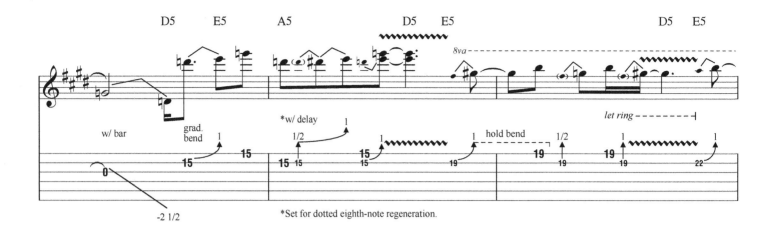

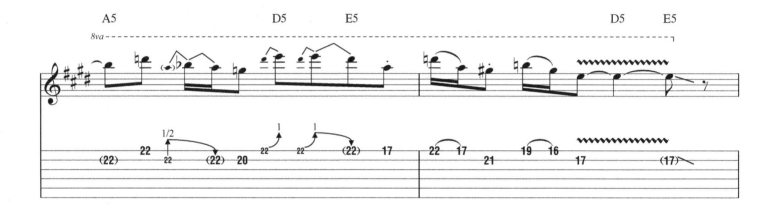

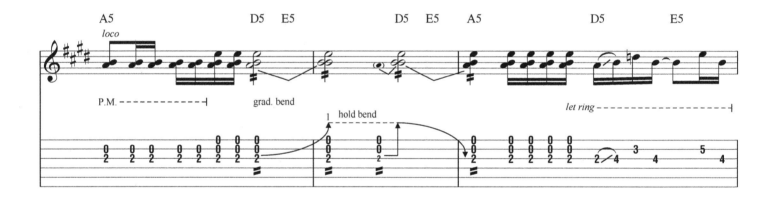

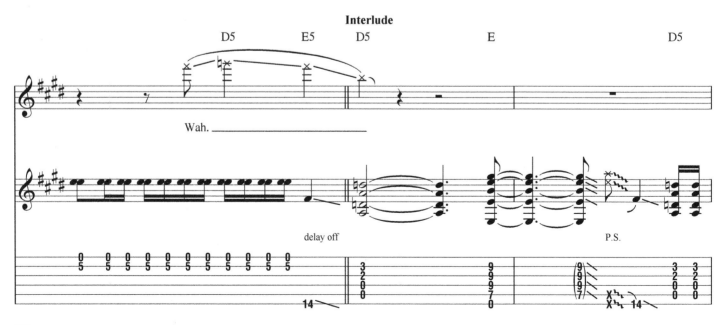

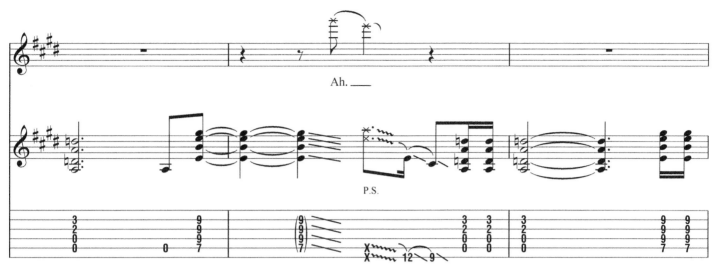

E   D5   E

Ah. ____

P.S.

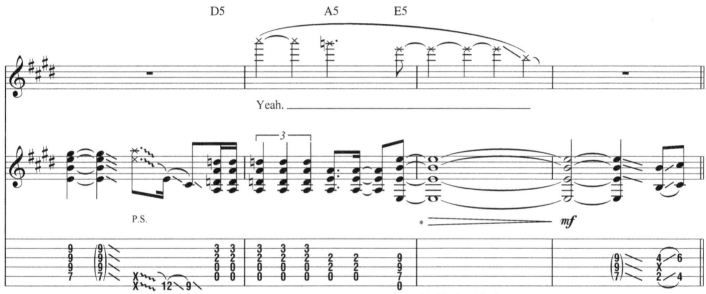

D5   A5 E5

Yeah. _____

P.S.

*Roll back vol. knob to 5.

Chorus

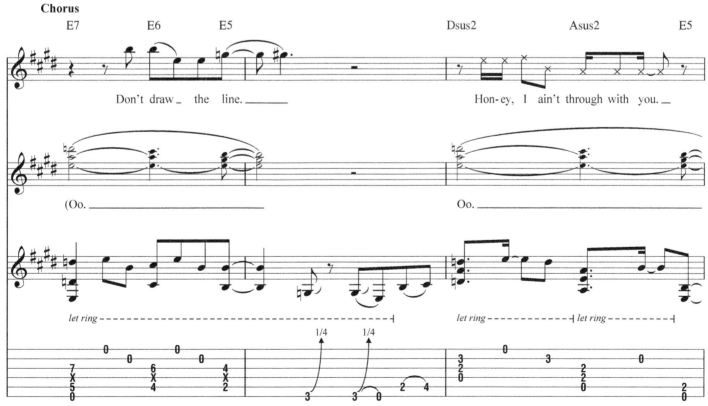

E7 E6 E5   Dsus2   Asus2   E5

Don't draw_ the line. _____   Hon-ey, I ain't through with you. __

(Oo. _____   Oo. ____

let ring ---------------------------------- let ring -------------- let ring ------------

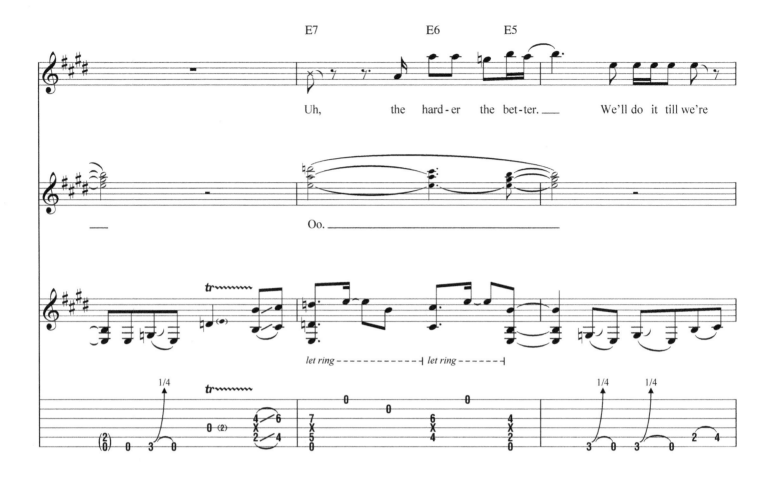

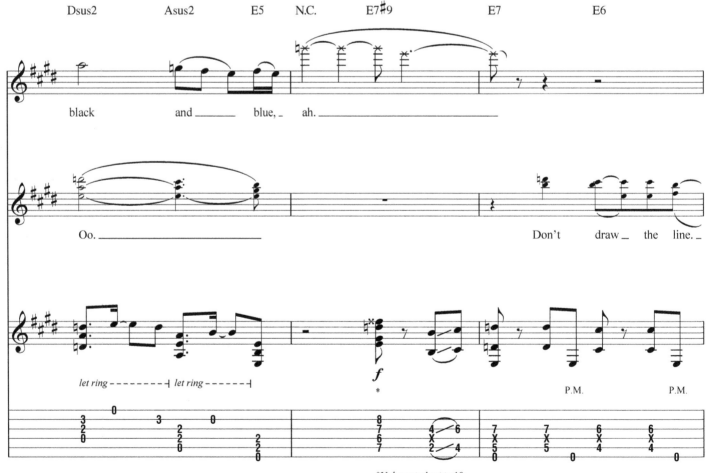

*Vol. control set to 10.

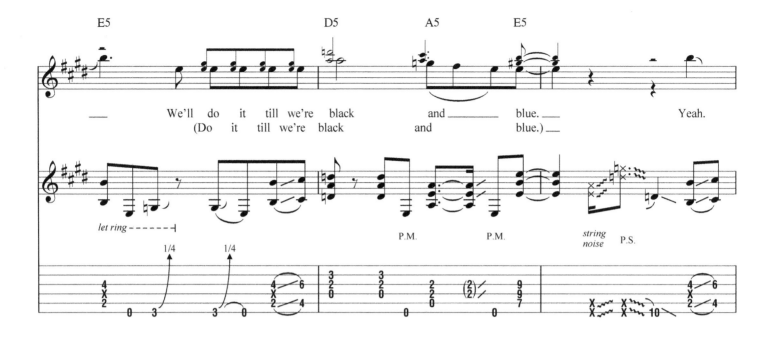

We'll do it till we're black and ___ blue. ___ Yeah.
(Do it till we're black and blue.) ___

The wet-ter the bet-ter, ___ we'll do it till we're black and ___ blue, ___
(Black and blue. ___

___ yeah, ___ uh.

Hoo, hoo, hoo, hoo, Do it till we're

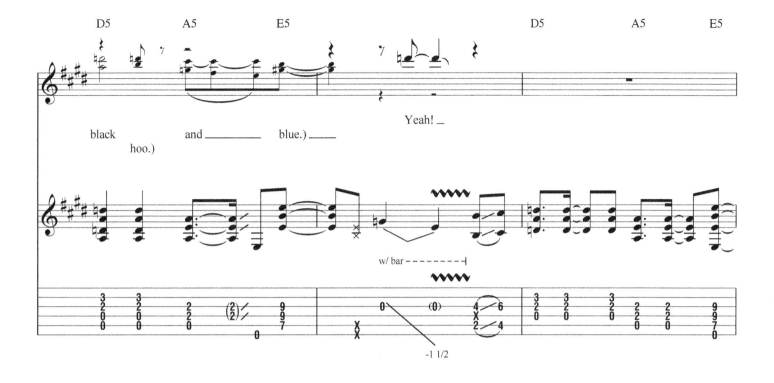

black   and _____ blue.) _____
hoo.)

Yeah! _

w/ bar ------------|

-1 1/2

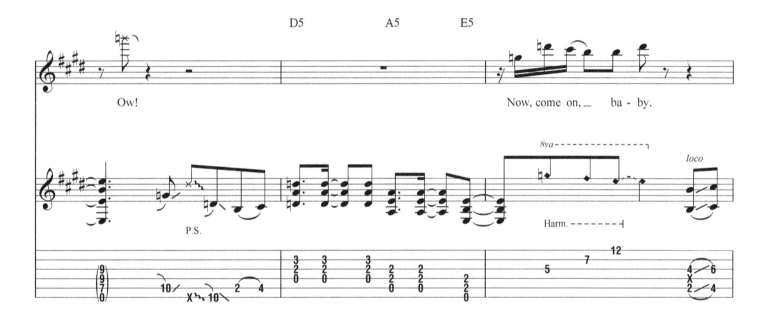

Ow!

Now, come on, _ ba - by.

8va --------------------|

loco

P.S.

Harm. ---------|

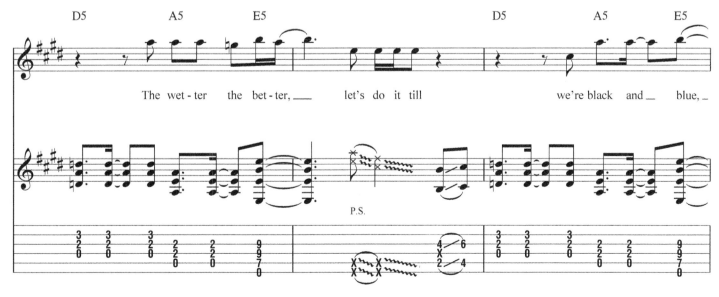

The wet - ter the bet - ter, ___ let's do it till   we're black and _ blue, _

P.S.

Outro

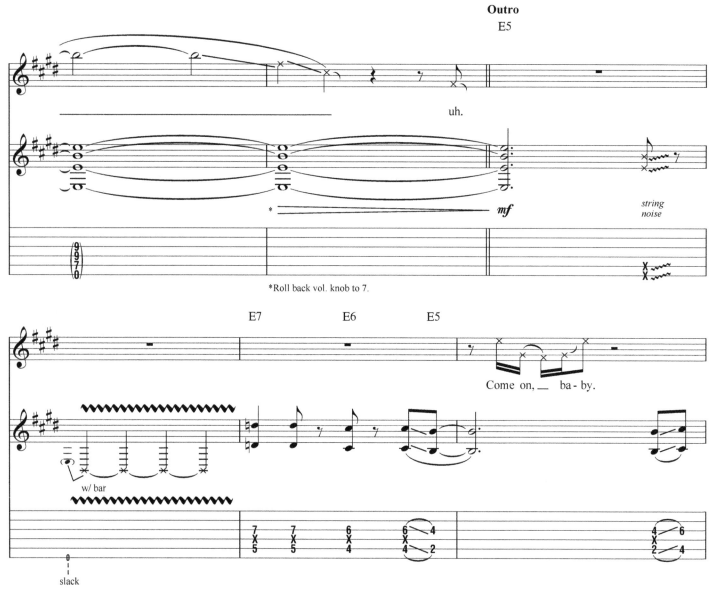

*Roll back vol. knob to 7.

Come on, __ ba - by.

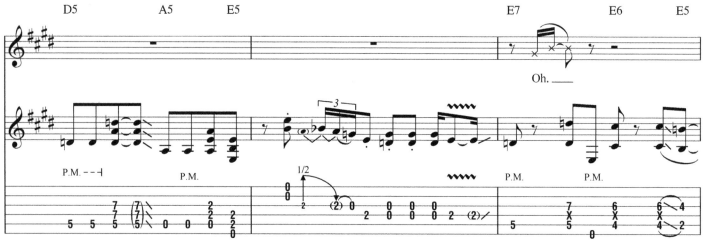

Oh. ____

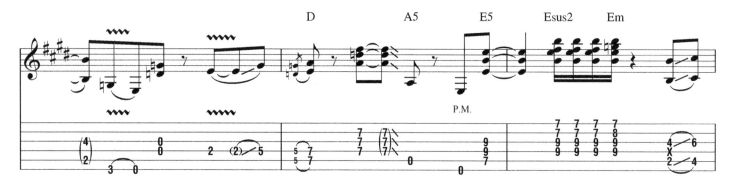

Uh.

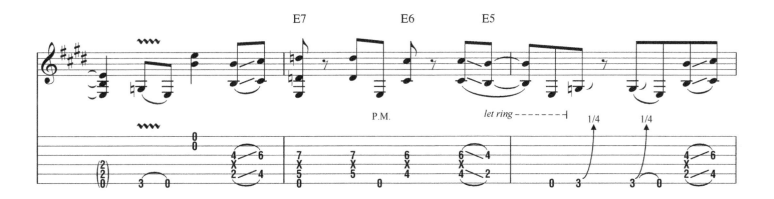

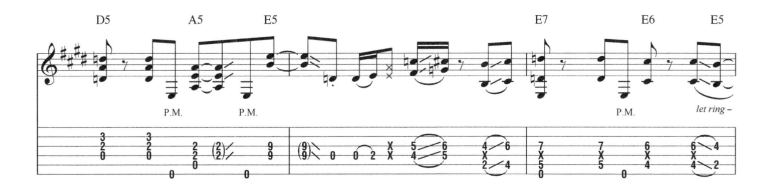

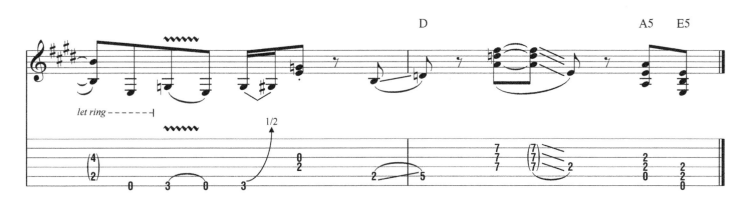

Can't Stop Loving You

Words and Music by Edward Van Halen, Alex Van Halen, Michael Anthony and Sammy Hagar

*Chord symbols reflect basic harmony.

**Tapped harmonics produced by fretting lower note,
then tapping at fret indicated in parentheses.

Verse

*Thumb on 6th string where applicable.

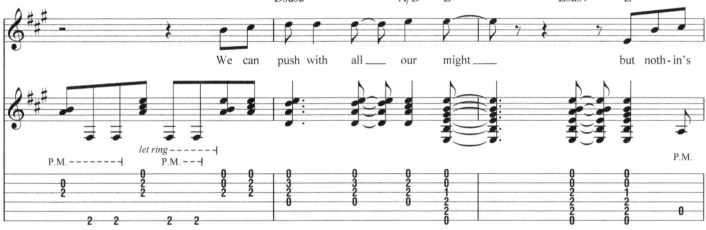

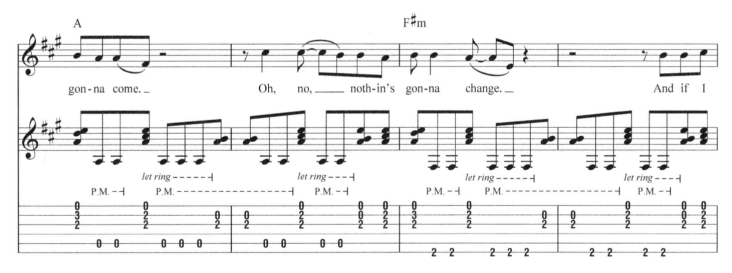

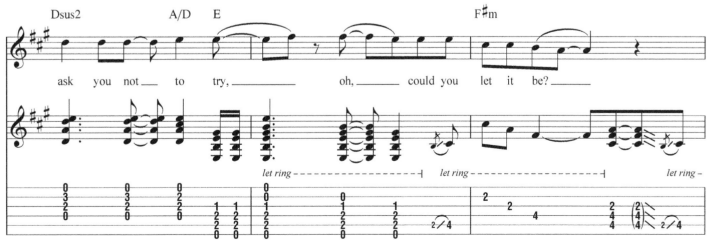

31

Pre-Chorus

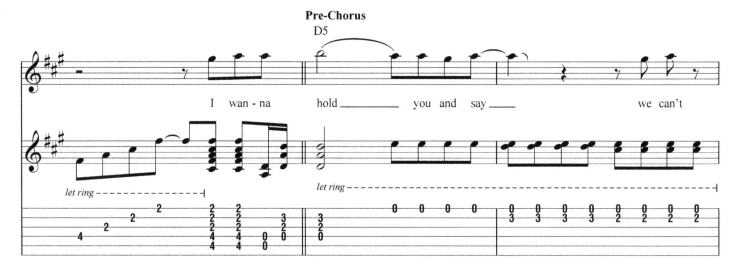

I wan-na hold _____ you and say _____ we can't

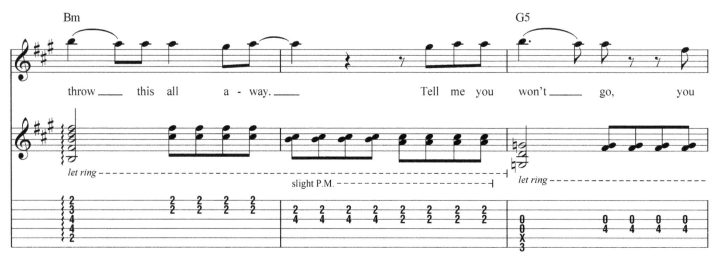

throw _____ this all a - way. _____ Tell me you won't _____ go, you

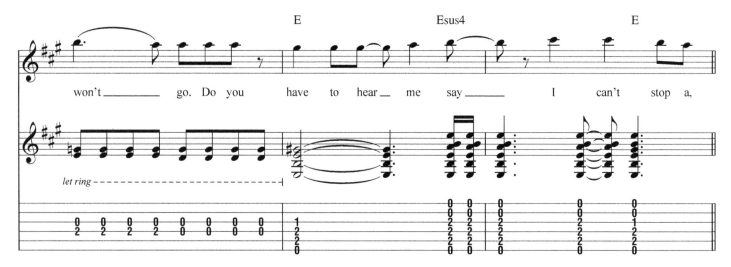

won't _____ go. Do you have to hear _ me say _____ I can't stop a,

Chorus

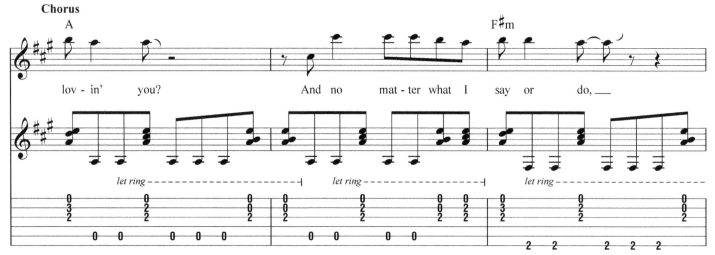

lov - in' you? And no mat - ter what I say or do, _____

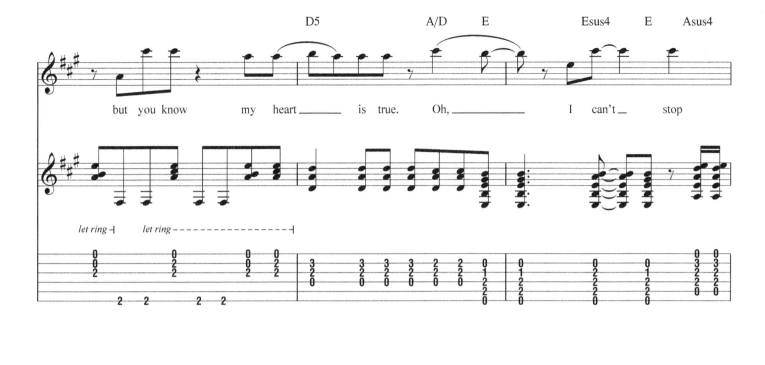

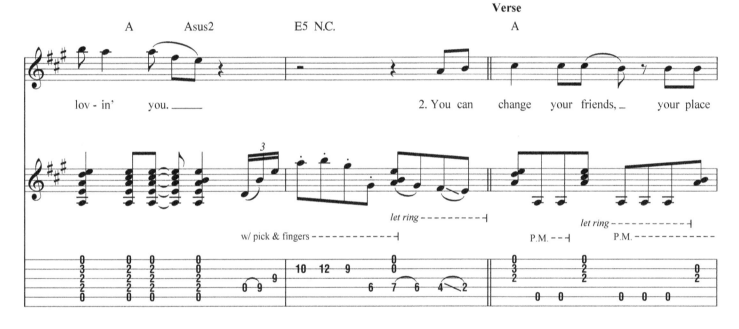

33

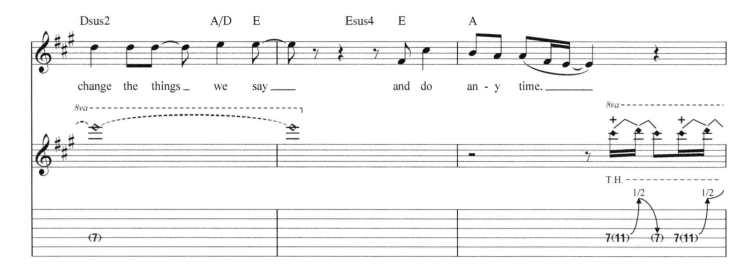

change the things ___ we say ___ and do an-y time. ___

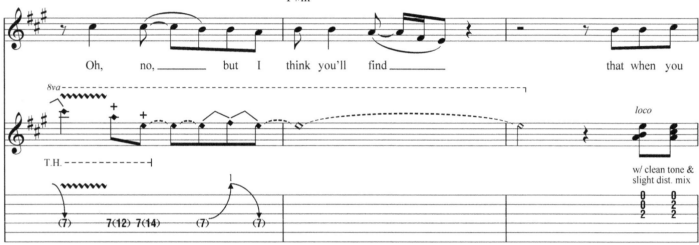

Oh, no, ___ but I think you'll find ___ that when you

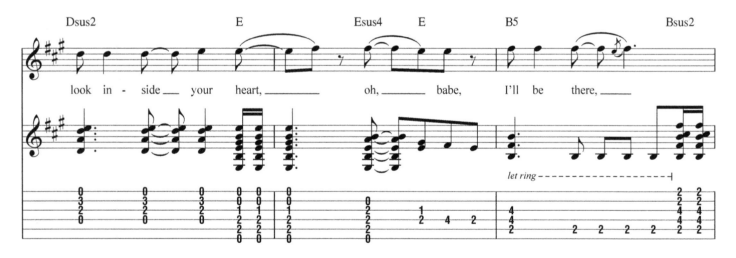

look in-side ___ your heart, ___ oh, ___ babe, I'll be there, ___

Pre-Chorus

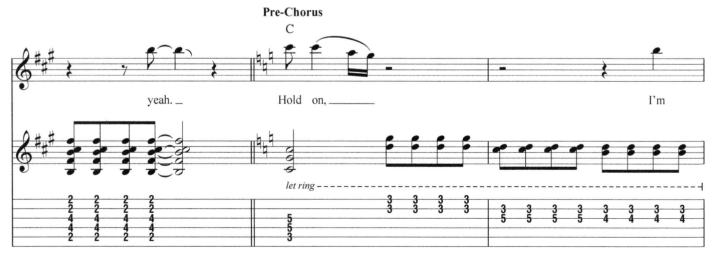

yeah. ___ Hold on, ___ I'm

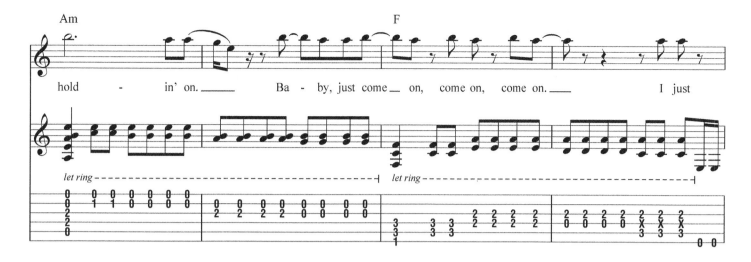

Am   F

hold - in' on. _____ Ba - by, just come _ on, come on, come on. _____ I just

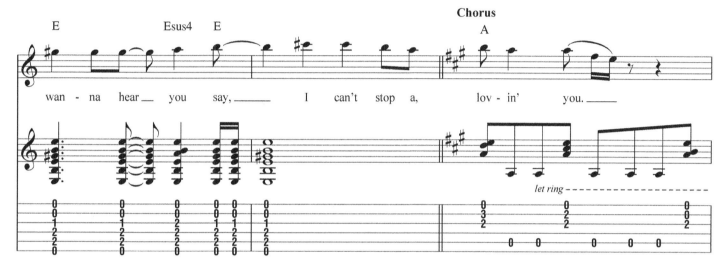

E   Esus4   E   **Chorus**
                           A

wan - na hear _ you say, _____ I can't stop a, lov - in' you. _____

F#m

And no mat - ter what you say or do, ___ you know _____ my

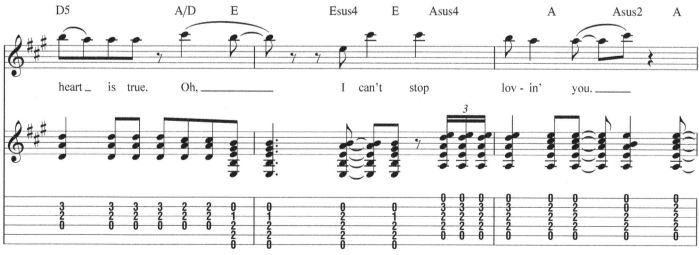

D5   A/D   E   Esus4   E   Asus4   A   Asus2   A

heart _ is true. Oh, _____ I can't stop lov - in' you. _____

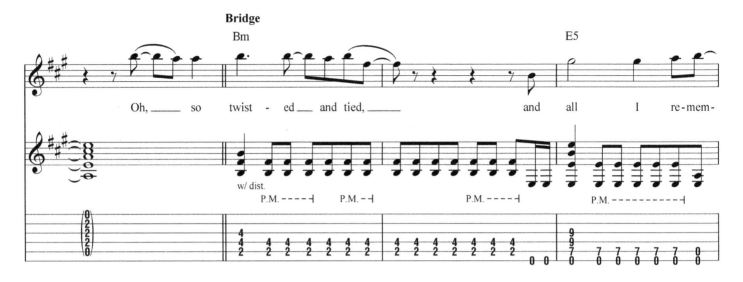

Bridge

Bm

E5

Oh, _____ so twist - ed _____ and tied, _____ and all I re - mem-

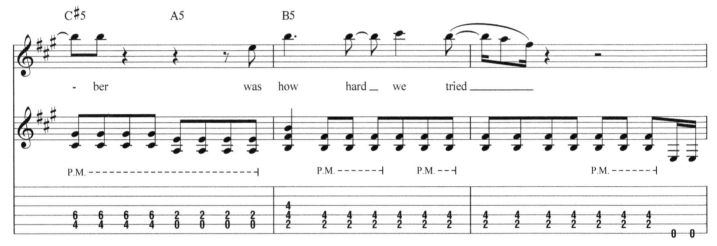

C#5

A5

B5

- ber was how hard _ we tried _____

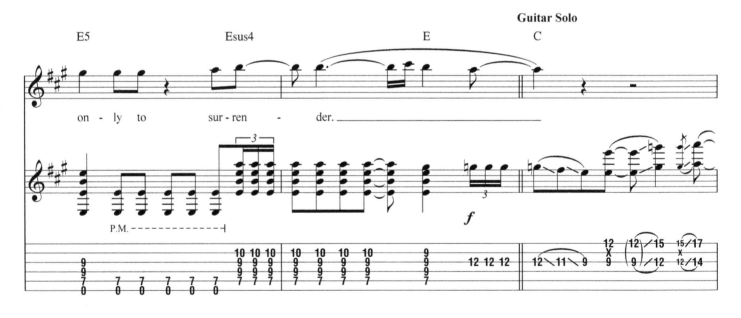

Guitar Solo

E5

Esus4

E

C

on - ly to sur - ren - der. _____

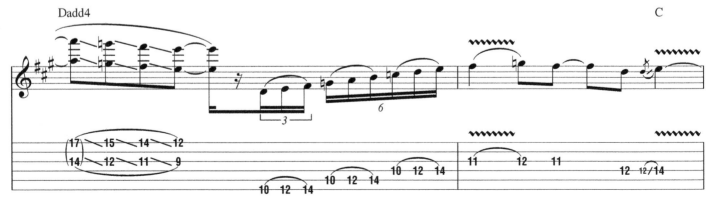

Dadd4

C

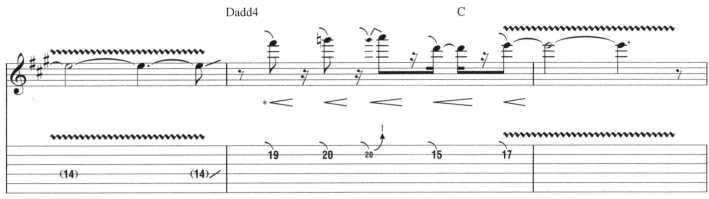

*Vol. swells

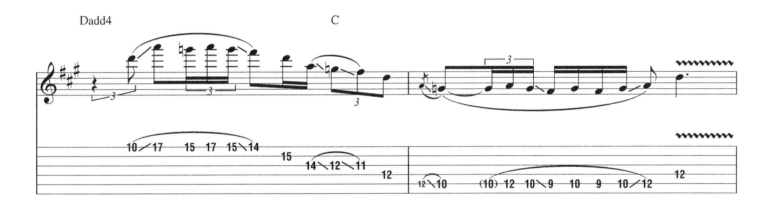

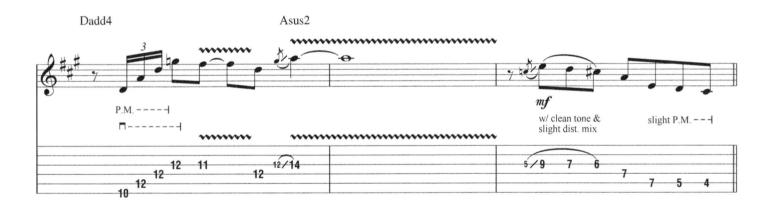

Verse

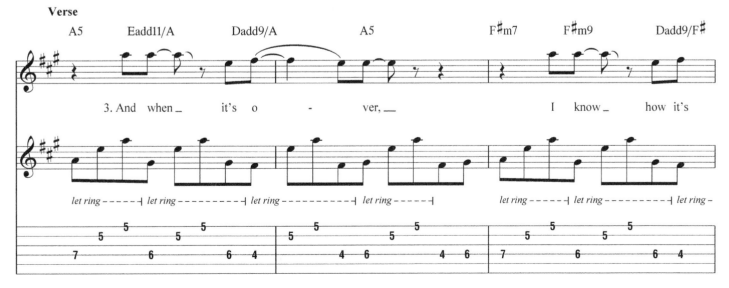

3. And when it's o - ver, I know how it's

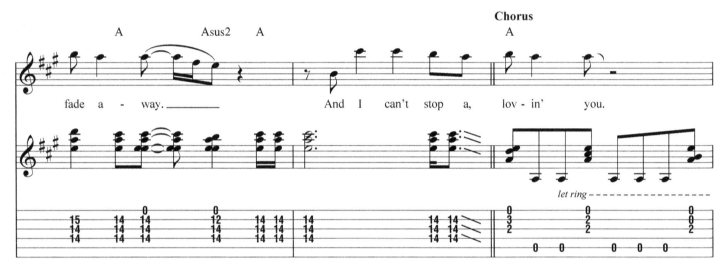

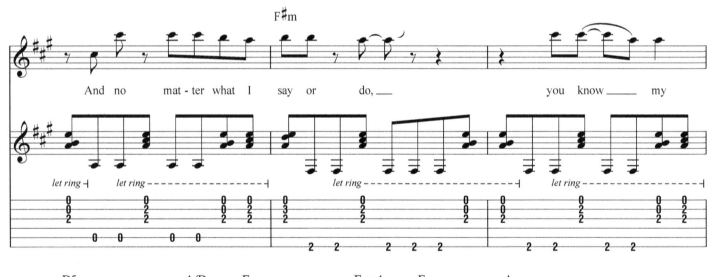

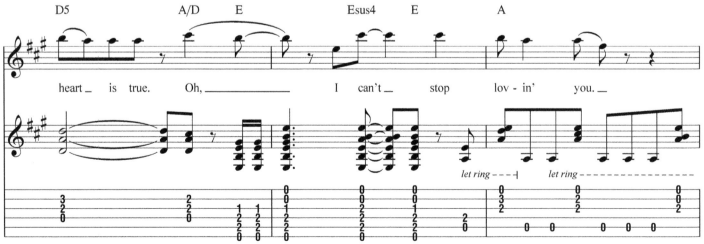

And I know _____ what I got to do. _____ Hey, Ray! What you said _

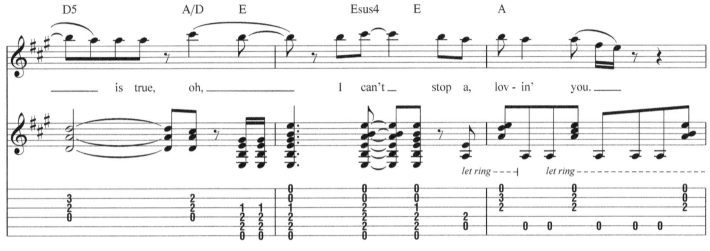

_____ is true, oh, _____ I can't _ stop a, lov - in' you. _____

Oh, _____ no. _____ Oh,

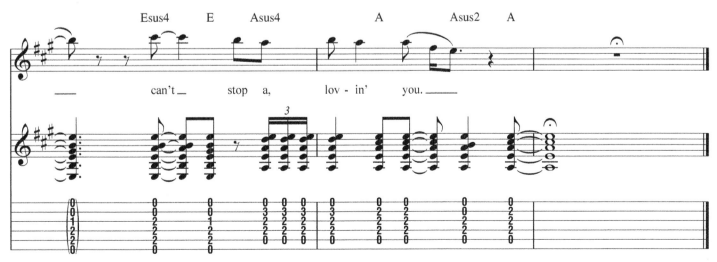

_____ can't _ stop a, lov - in' you. _____

Dreams

Words and Music by Edward Van Halen, Alex Van Halen, Michael Anthony and Sammy Hagar

Intro
Moderately fast ♩ = 140

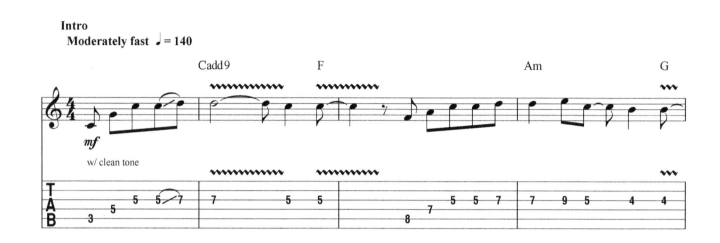

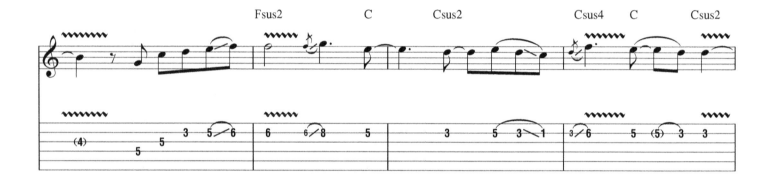

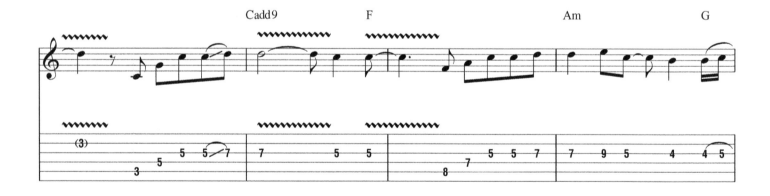

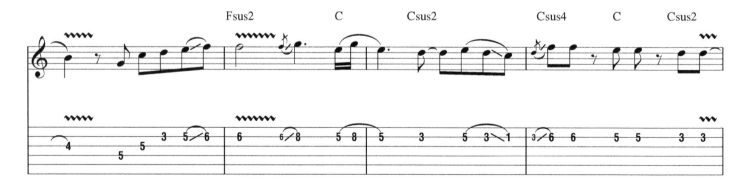

1. World turns black and white,

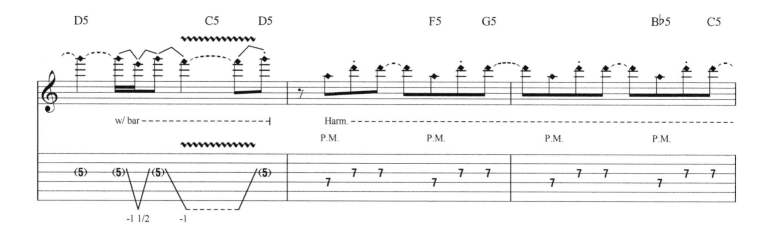

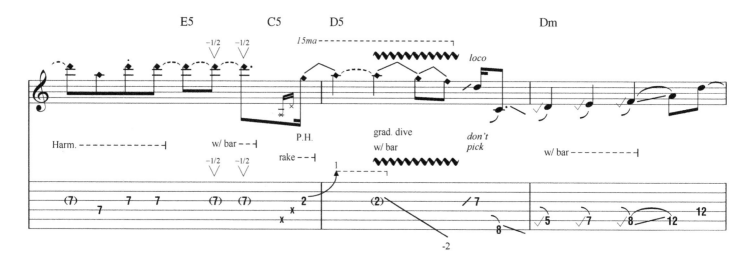

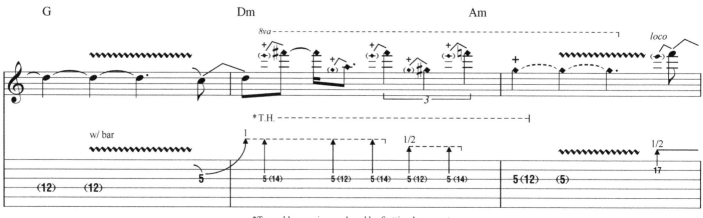

*Tapped harmonics produced by fretting lower note,
then tapping at fret indicated in parentheses.

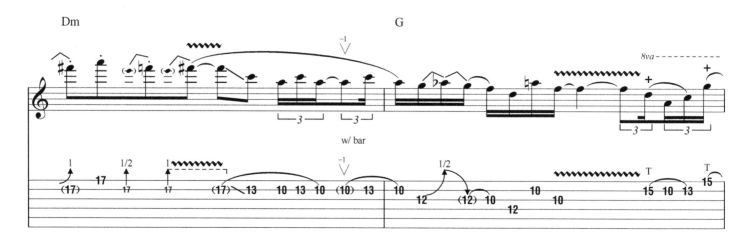

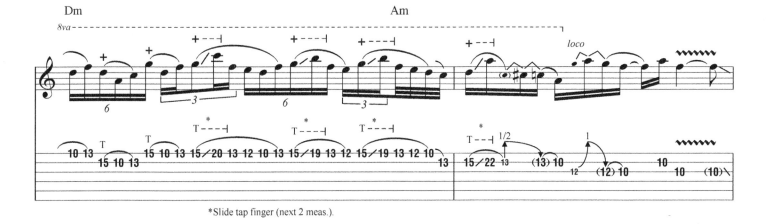

*Slide tap finger (next 2 meas.).

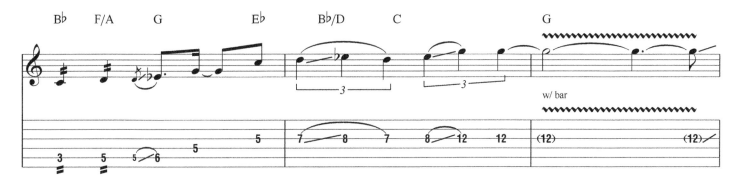

Chorus

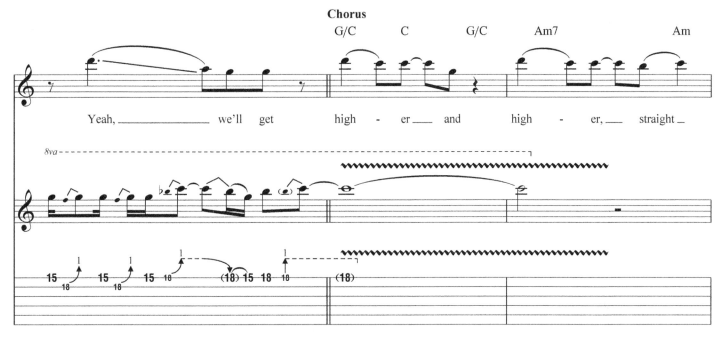

Yeah, _____ we'll get high - er ___ and high - er, ___ straight ___ up we'll climb. ___

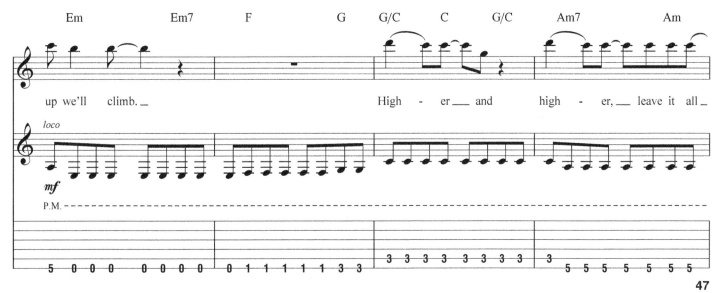

High - er ___ and high - er, ___ leave it all ___

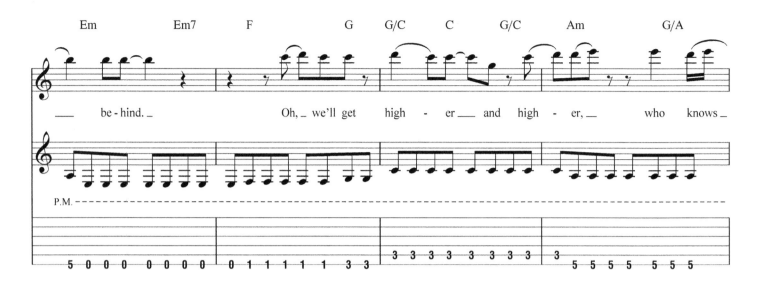

be-hind.　　Oh, _ we'll get high - er _ and high - er, _ who knows _

⊕ Coda 2

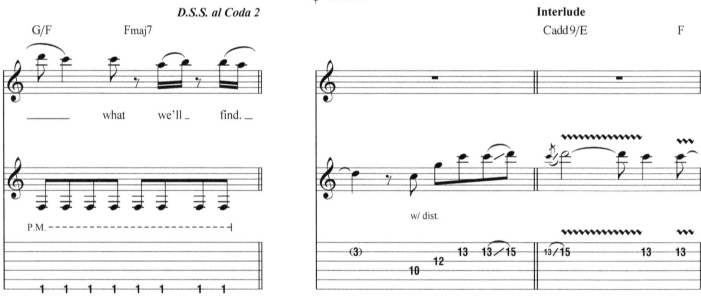

D.S.S. al Coda 2

G/F　Fmaj7

what　we'll _ find. _

Interlude

Cadd9/E　F

w/ dist.

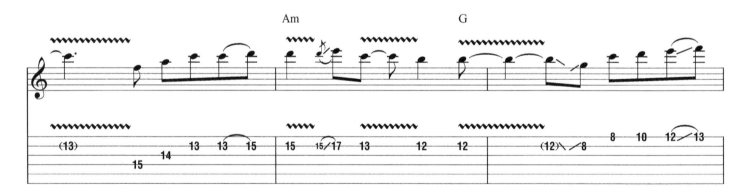

Am　G

Fsus2　Am7　Am7add4

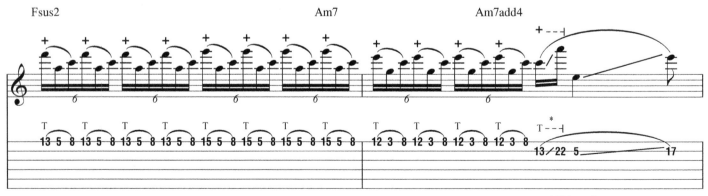

*Slide tap finger.

Finish What Ya Started

Words and Music by Edward Van Halen, Alex Van Halen, Michael Anthony and Sammy Hagar

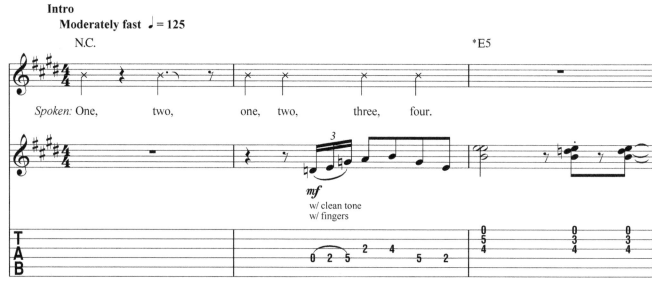

Spoken: One, two, one, two, three, four.

w/ clean tone
w/ fingers

*Chord symbols reflect basic harmony.

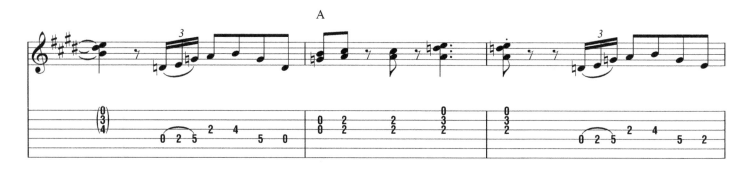

Come on, ba - by.

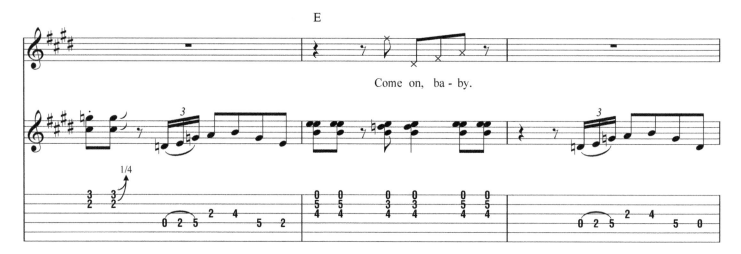

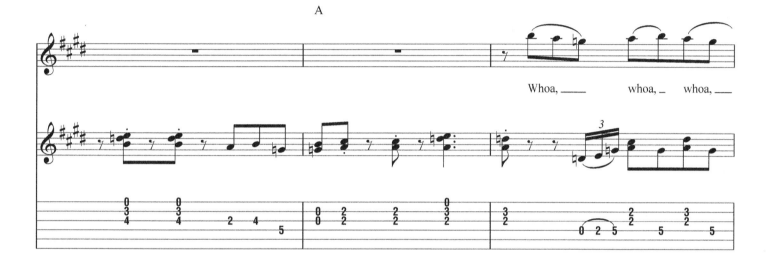

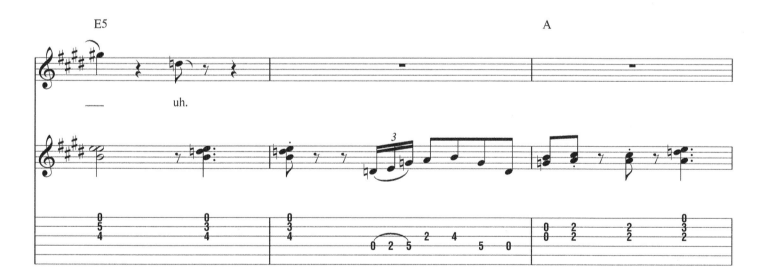

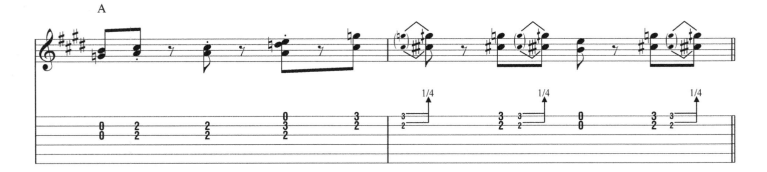

Verse

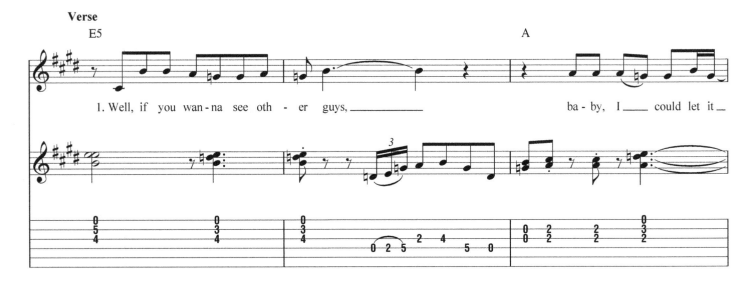

1. Well, if you wan-na see oth - er guys, _____ ba - by, I ___ could let it ___ ___ slide. _____ You want a lov - er, you want a friend, ma - ma, I can be both of them. _____

Pre-Chorus

I got the tools

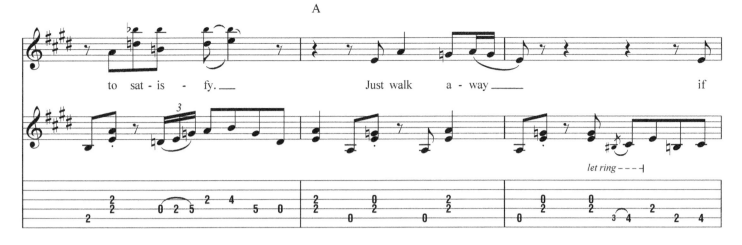

A

to sat - is - fy.＿ Just walk a - way＿ if

C#m

D5

I fall＿ shy＿ at all,＿ uh.

Chorus

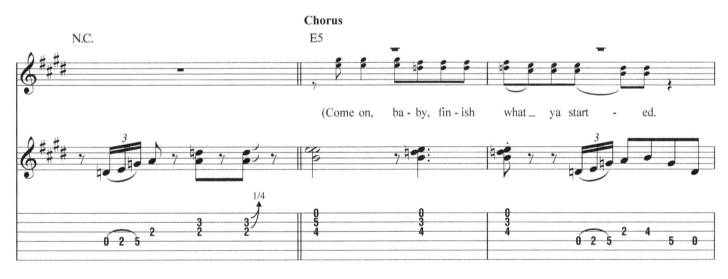

N.C.

E5

(Come on, ba - by, fin - ish what＿ ya start - ed.

A

E5

I'm in - com - plete,＿ uh.

That ain't no way to treat the

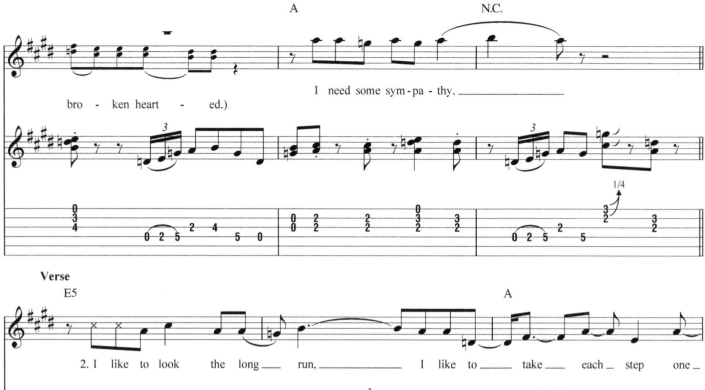

I need some sym-pa-thy. _____

bro - ken heart - ed.)

Verse

2. I like to look the long ___ run, _____ I like to ___ take ___ each step one ___

___ by one. ___ Right on time you will ar - rive,

uh, ___ by keep-ing the dream ___ a - live. _____ Uh, it's a - live _____

_____ and it's kick-ing   in-side of me. _____   So

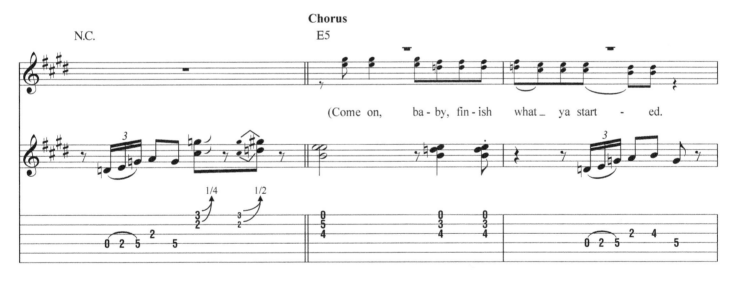

come   on, _____ ba - by,   please. _____

Chorus

(Come on,   ba - by, fin - ish   what _ ya start - ed.

Oh, I'm in - com-plete, _____   uh.

That ain't no way to treat the

A

Ow,___ come on and fin - ish me.___

bro - ken heart - ed. Fin - ish.)

Guitar Solo

F#5   G5   D   A5

(Ba - by, come on.___

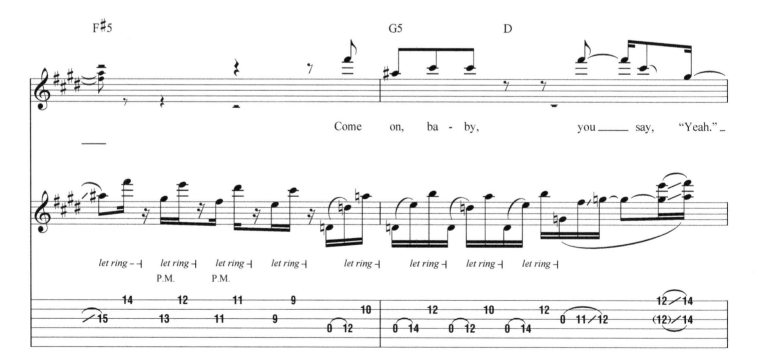

F#5   G5   D

Come on, ba - by, you___ say, "Yeah."___

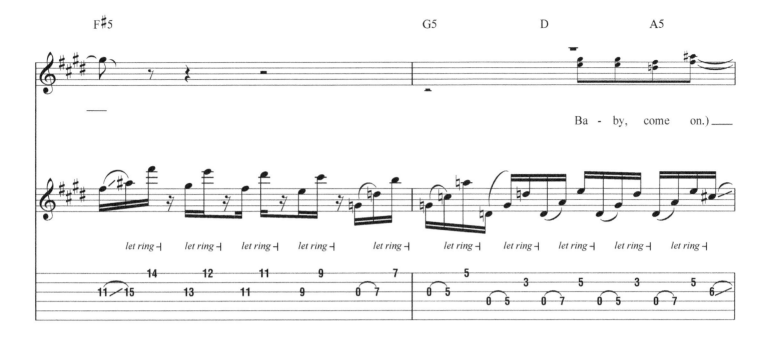

Ba - by, come on.) ____

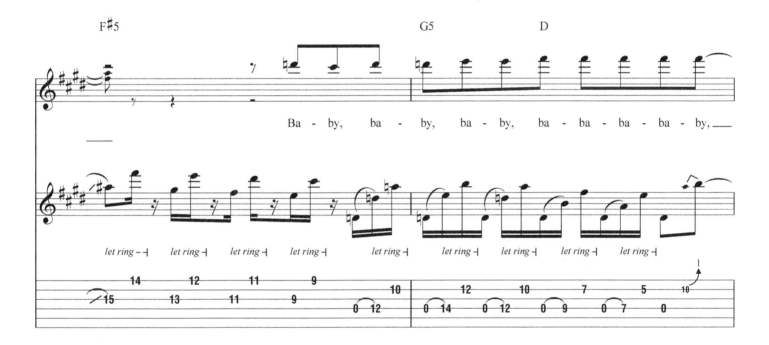

Ba - by, ba - by, ba - by, ba - ba - ba - ba - by, ____

yeah.

Interlude

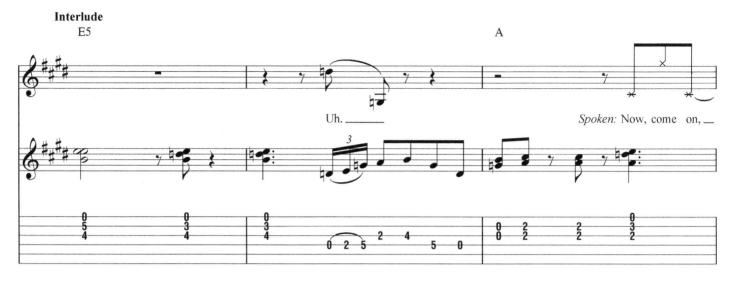

Uh. _____

Spoken: Now, come on, ___

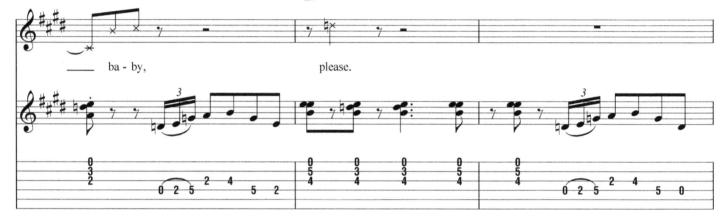

_____ ba - by,   please.

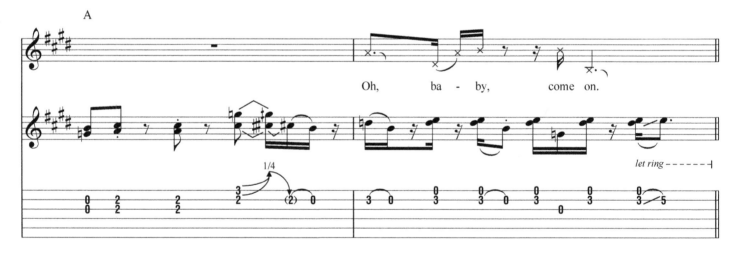

Oh,   ba - by,   come on.

Chorus

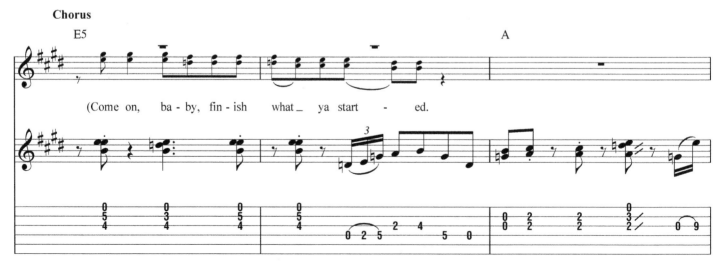

(Come on,   ba - by, fin - ish   what_ ya start - ed.

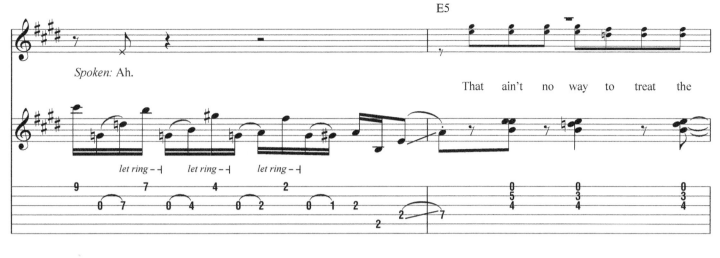

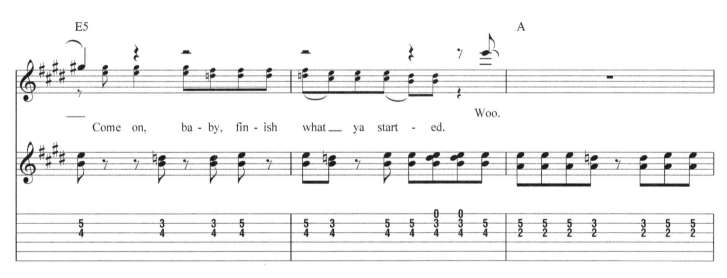

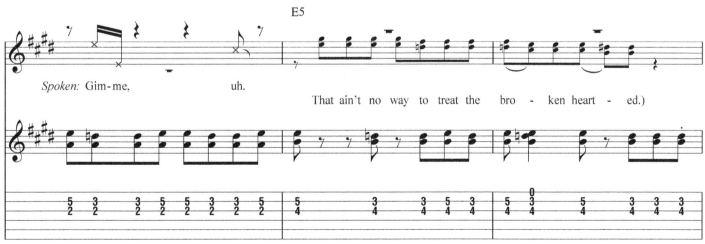

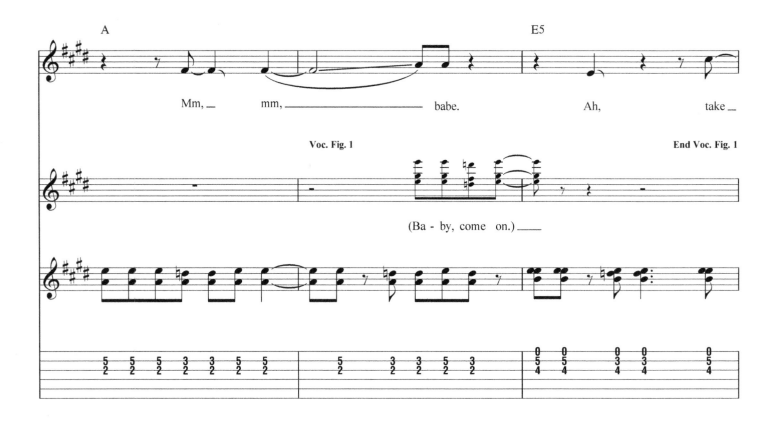

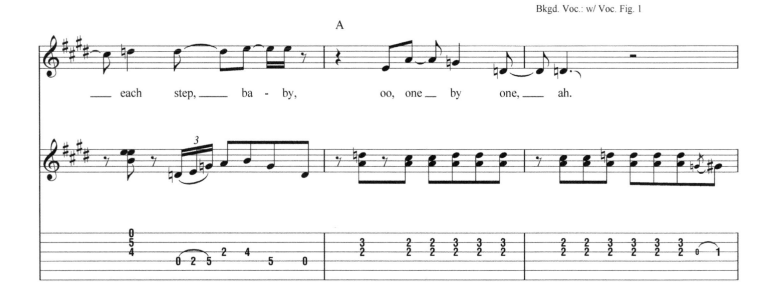

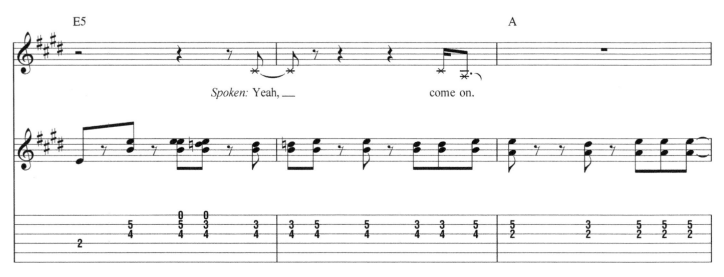

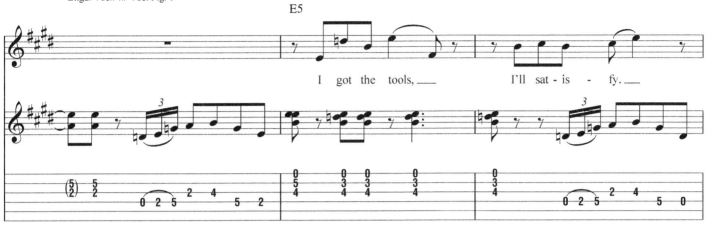

Bkgd. Voc.: w/ Voc. Fig. 1

I got the tools, ___ I'll sat - is - fy. ___

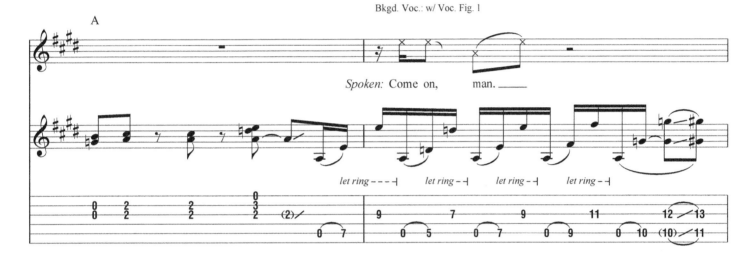

Bkgd. Voc.: w/ Voc. Fig. 1

Spoken: Come on, man. ___

Whoa, ___ whoa, ___ whoa, ___ yeah. ___

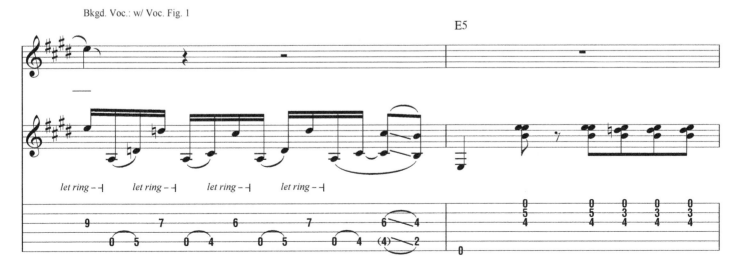

Bkgd. Voc.: w/ Voc. Fig. 1

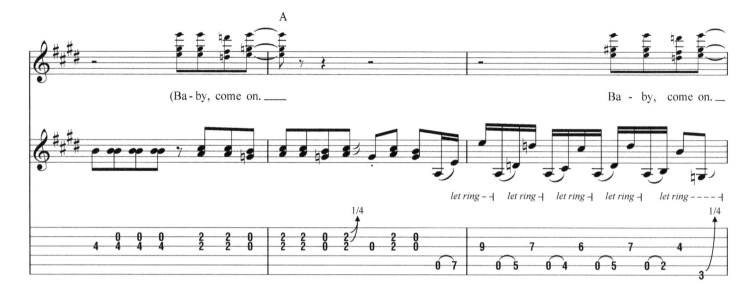

(Ba - by, come on. ____

Ba - by, come on. ____

Begin fade

So come on, ____ ba - by.

So come on, ____

Ba - by, come on. ____

Fade out

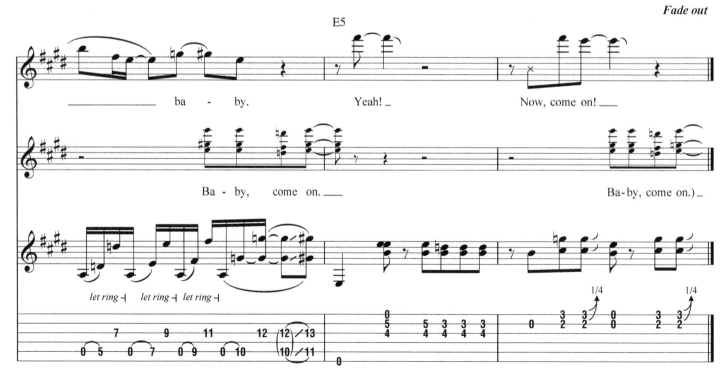

____ ba - by. Yeah! ____ Now, come on! ____

Ba - by,   come on. ____   Ba - by, come on.) ____

Right Now

Words and Music by Edward Van Halen, Alex Van Halen, Michael Anthony and Sammy Hagar

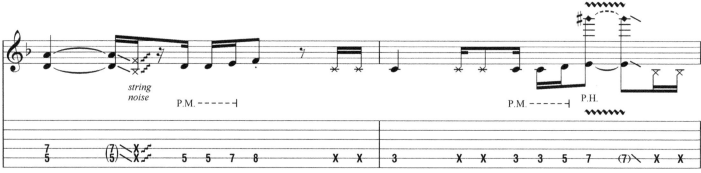

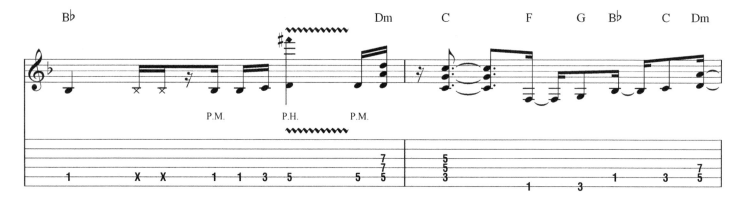

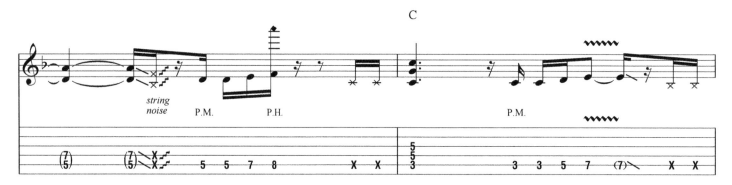

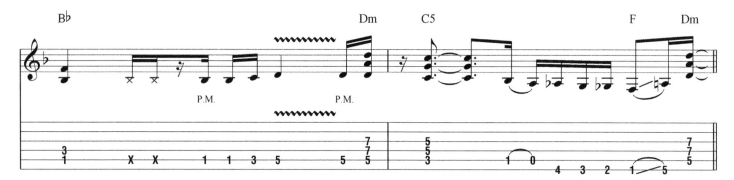

Verse

1. Don't wan-na wait till to-mor - row, why put it off an-oth-er day?

Pre-Chorus

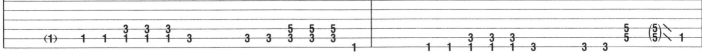

Make fu - ture plans, __ don't dream a - bout __ yes - ter-day, _____ hey.

Come on, turn, __ turn this thing a - round. __

(Right

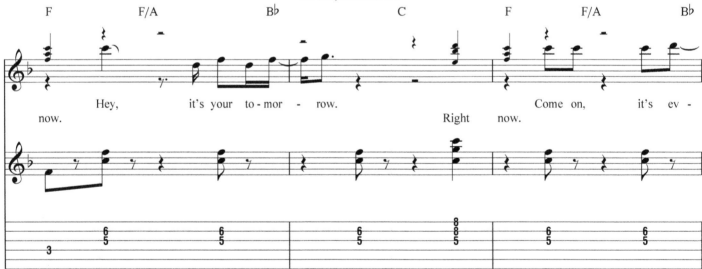

𝄋 **Chorus**

now.

Hey, it's your to - mor - row. Come on, it's ev -

Right now.

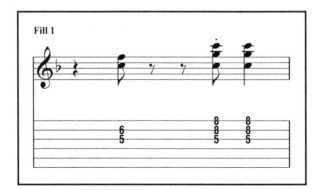

Fill 1

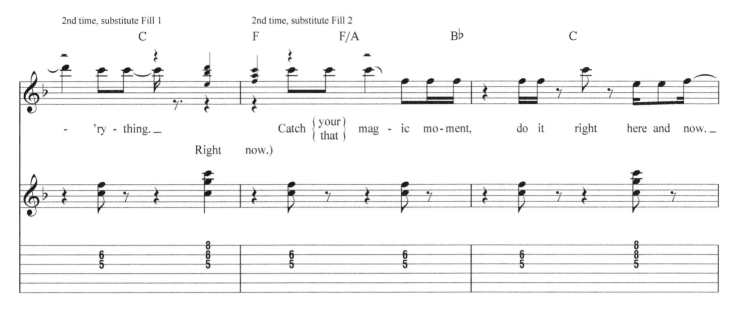

2nd time, substitute Fill 1   2nd time, substitute Fill 2

-'ry-thing.   Catch {your}{that} mag-ic mo-ment, do it right here and now.
(Right   now.)

To Coda

It means ev-'ry-thing.   2. Miss a beat, you lose the rhy-

w/ bar

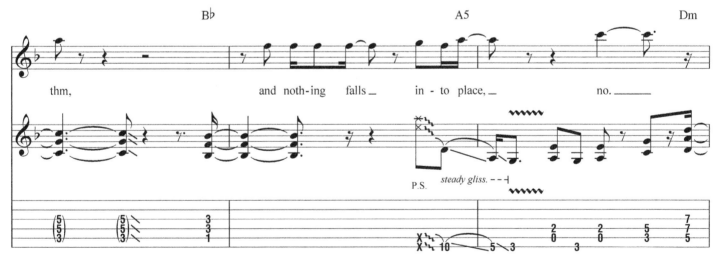

thm,   and noth-ing falls in-to place, no.

P.S.   *steady gliss.*

Fill 2

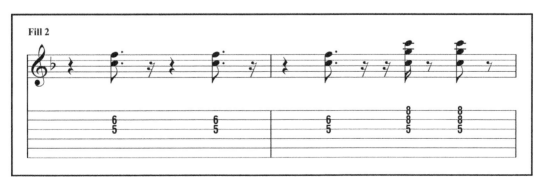

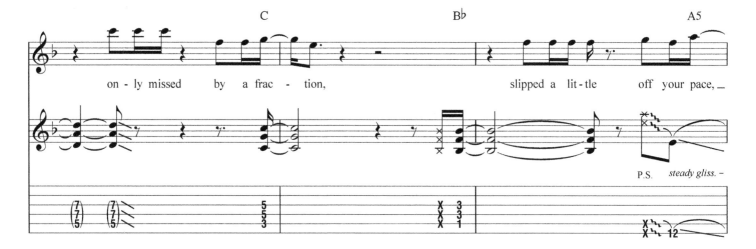

on - ly missed by a frac - tion, slipped a lit - tle off your pace,

Pre-Chorus

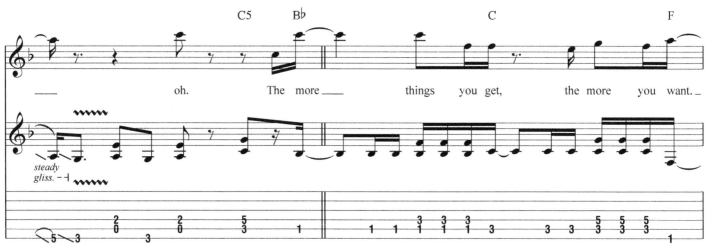

oh. The more ___ things you get, the more you want.

___ Just trade in one ___ for the oth-

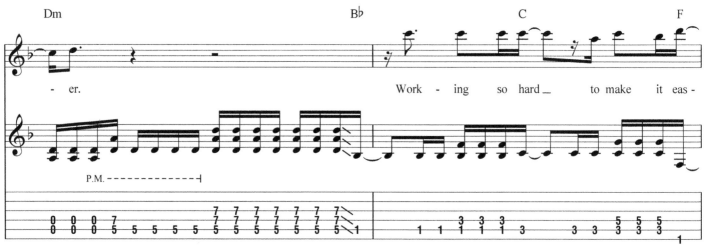

-er. Work - ing so hard ___ to make it eas-

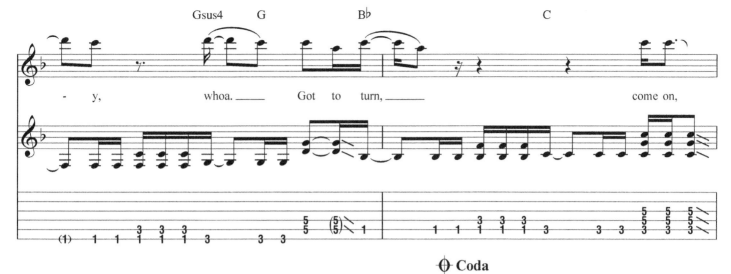

-y, whoa.____ Got to turn,____ come on,

Coda

D.S. al Coda

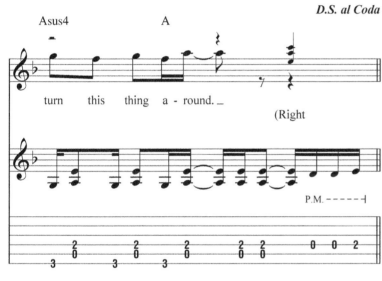

turn this thing a - round.__

(Right

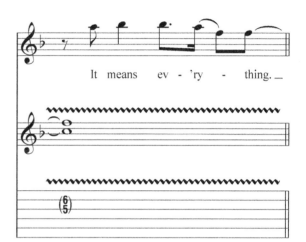

It means ev - 'ry - thing.__

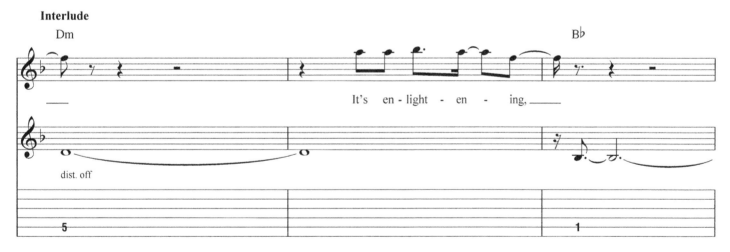

It's en - light - en - ing,____

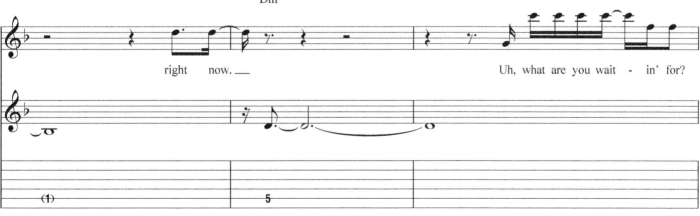

right now.__ Uh, what are you wait - in' for?

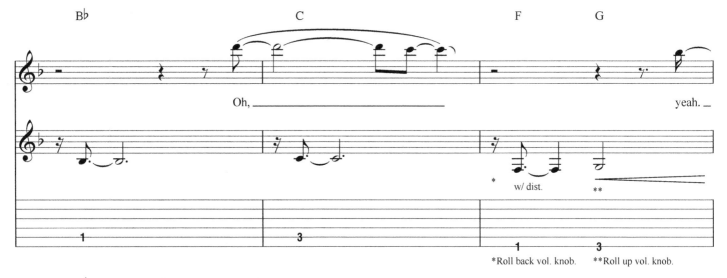

Oh, _____ yeah. __

*Roll back vol. knob.   **Roll up vol. knob.

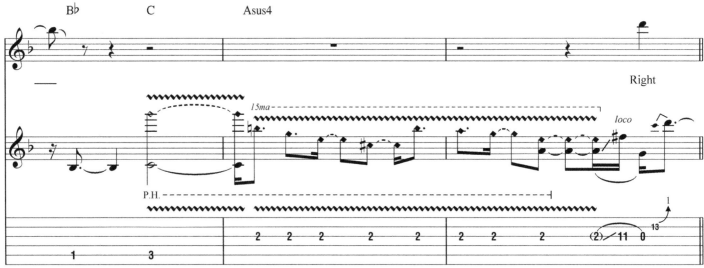

Right

Guitar Solo

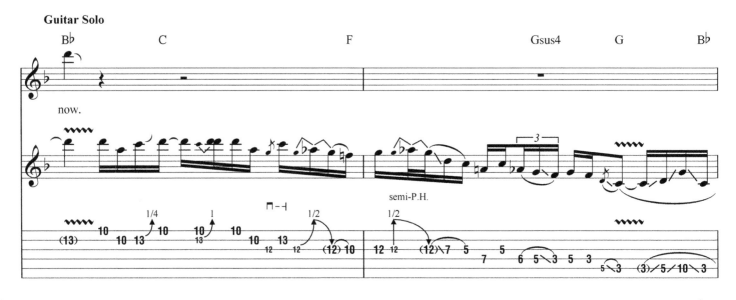

now.

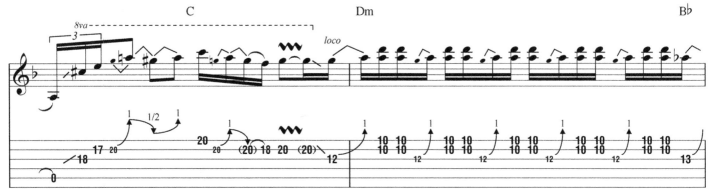

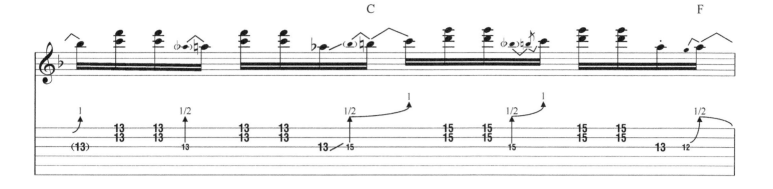

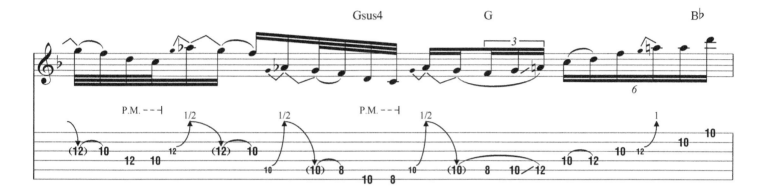

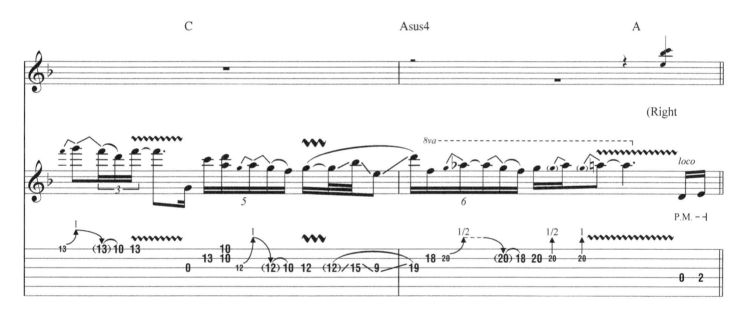

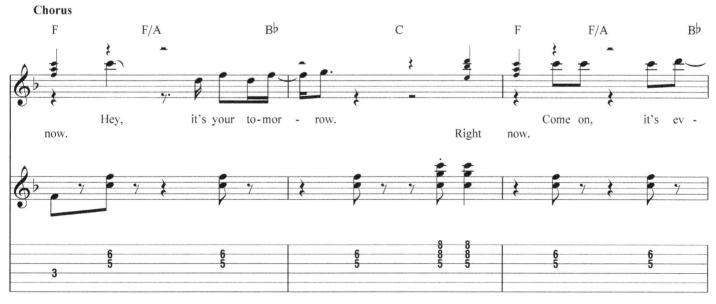

-'ry - thing. _ Catch that mag - ic mo - ment, do it right here and now. _
Right now. Right

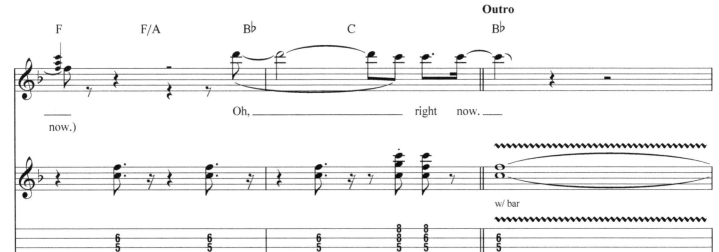

Outro

_____ Oh, _____ right now. ____
now.)

w/ bar

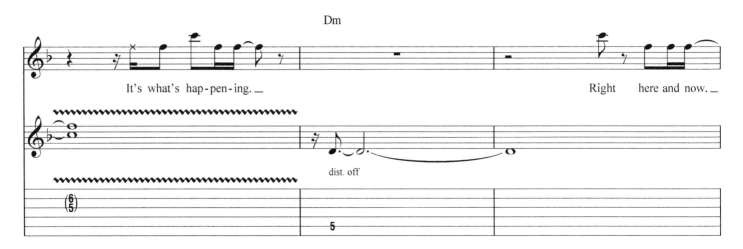

It's what's hap-pen-ing. _ Right here and now. _

dist. off

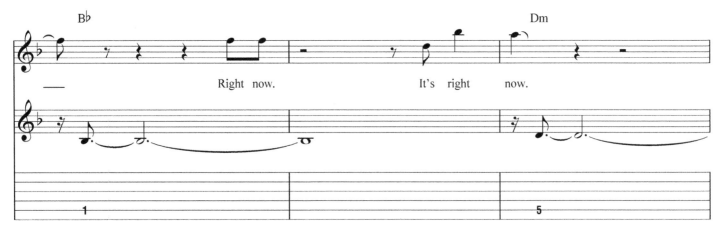

_____ Right now. It's right now.

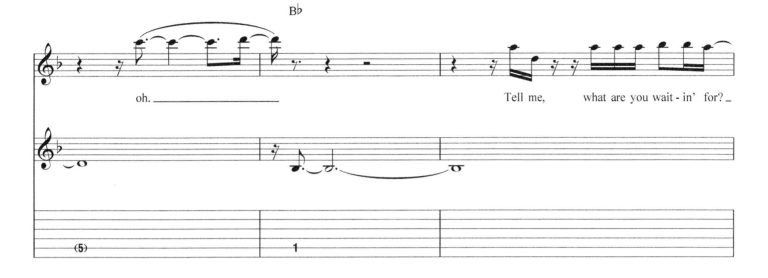

oh. _____ Tell me, what are you wait-in' for?_

Begin fade

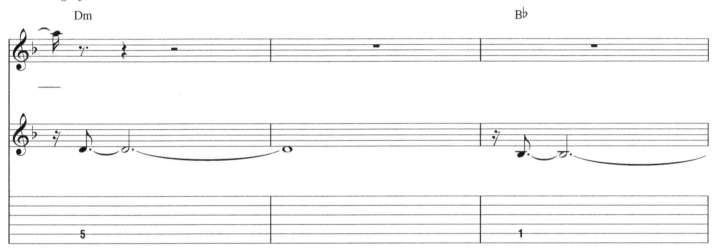

Turn this_ thing a-round.

Fade out

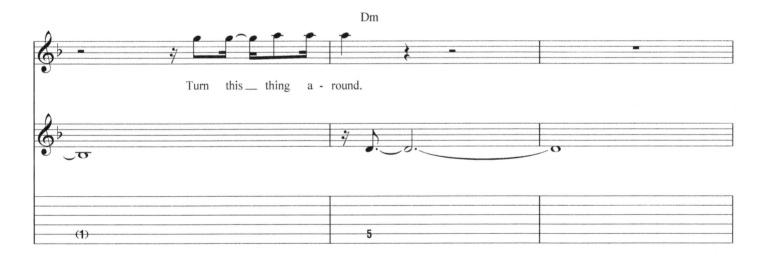

Top of the World

Words and Music by Edward Van Halen, Alex Van Halen, Michael Anthony and Sammy Hagar

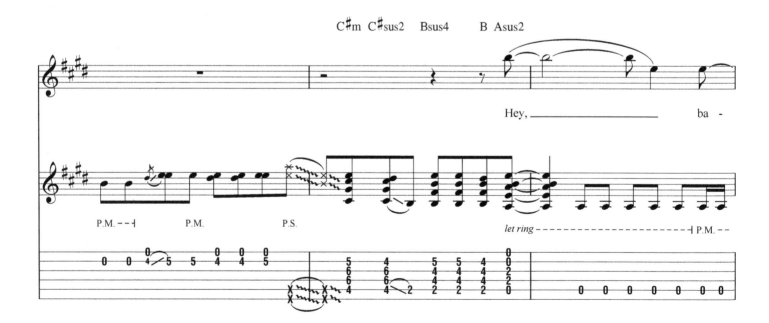

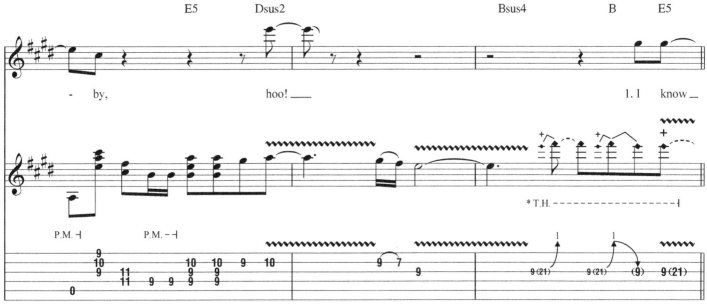

E5　Dsus2　　　　　Bsus4　B　E5

-by,　　　hoo! ___　　　　　　　　1. I　know ___

*Tapped harmonics produced by fretting lower note,
then tapping at fret indicated in parentheses.

Verse

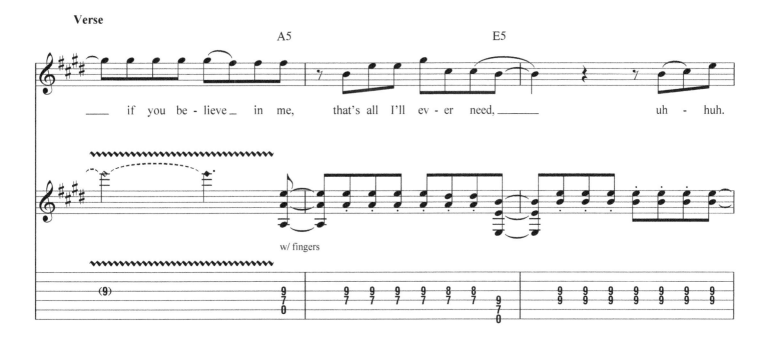

A5　　　　　　　　E5

___ if you be-lieve _ in me,　that's all I'll ev-er need, _____　uh-huh.

w/ fingers

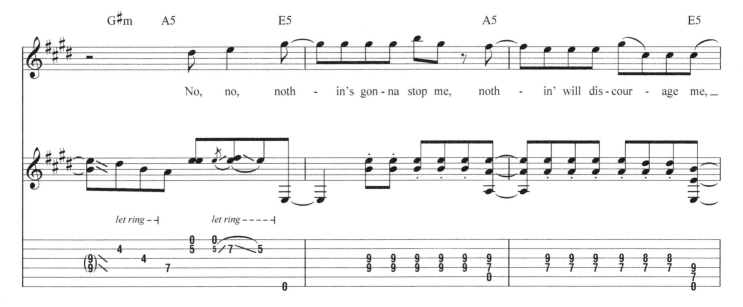

G#m　A5　　　　E5　　　　　　　A5　　　　　　　E5

No,　no,　noth-in's gon-na stop me,　noth-in' will dis-cour-age me, _

let ring ⌐⌐⌐⌐　let ring ⌐⌐⌐⌐⌐

Chorus

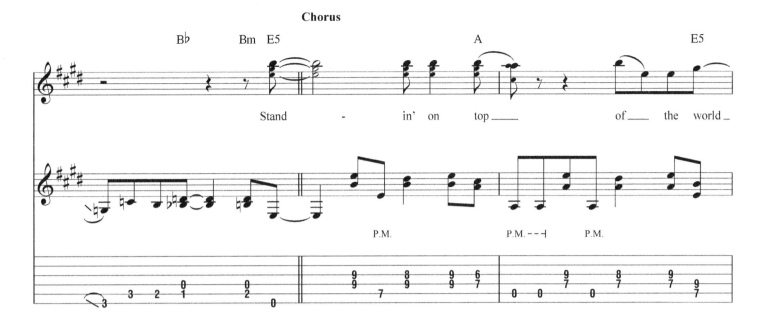

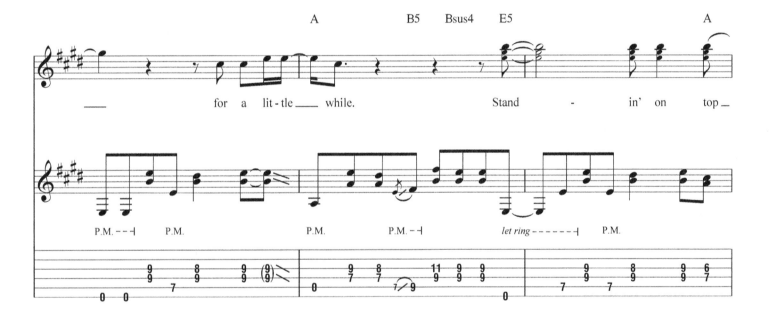

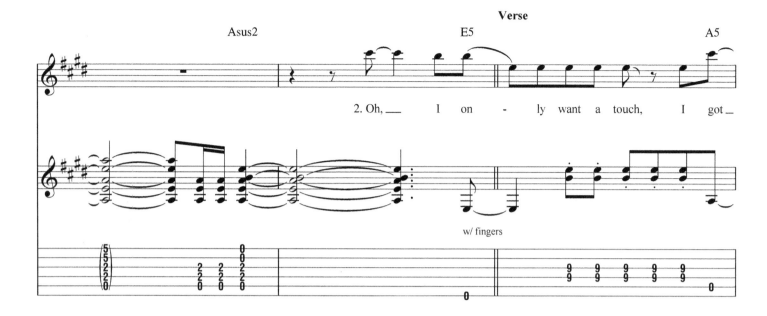

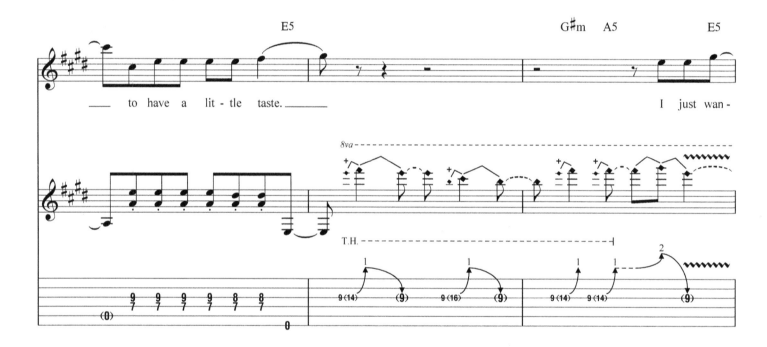

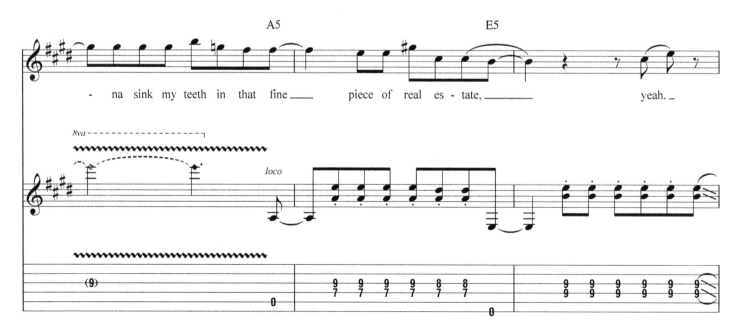

Hey, _____ ba - by, whoo, _

_____ make it nice___ and sweet. Oo. Oh, _____ lit - tle dar -

- lin', let's take a walk down Eas - y Street. Stand-

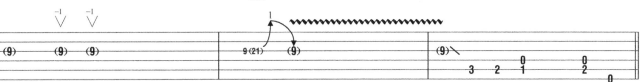

Chorus

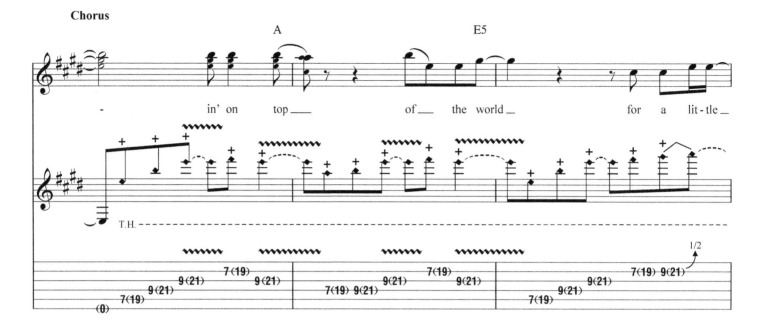

-in' on top ___ of ___ the world ___ for a lit-tle ___

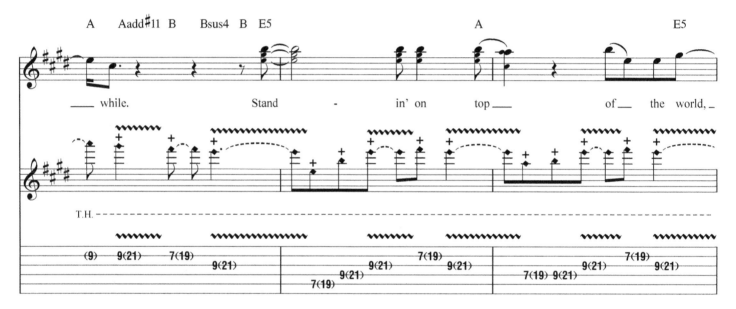

___ while. Stand - in' on top ___ of ___ the world, ___

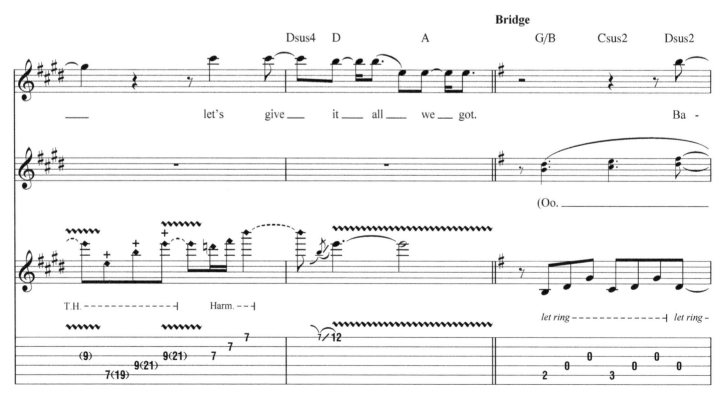

___ let's give ___ it ___ all ___ we ___ got. Ba -

(Oo. ___)

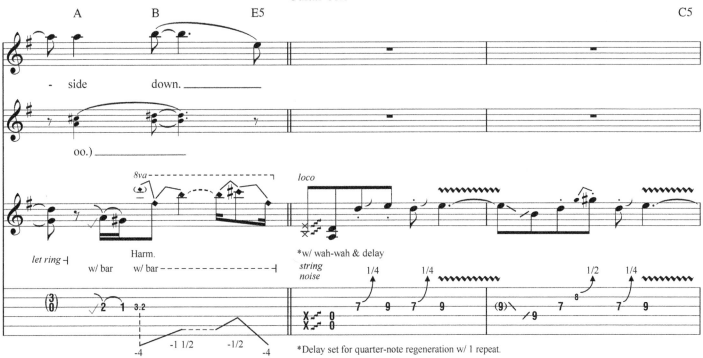

*Delay set for quarter-note regeneration w/ 1 repeat.

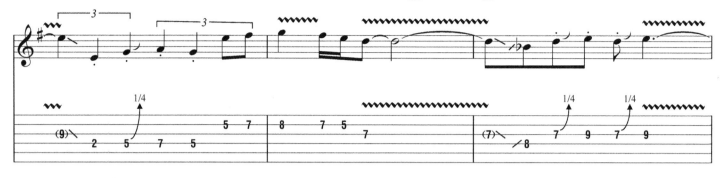

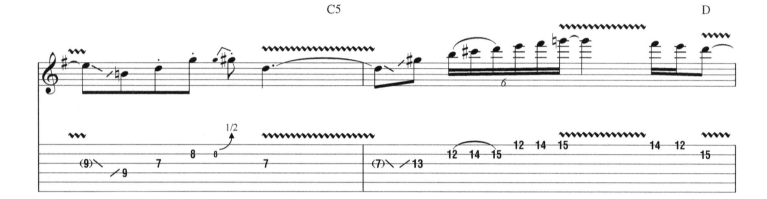

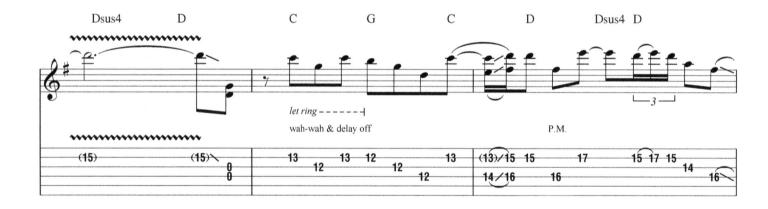

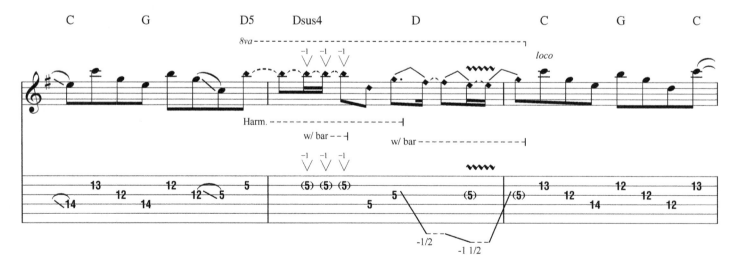

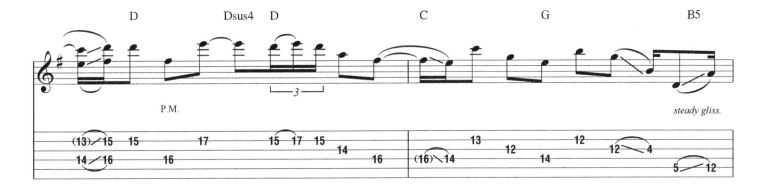

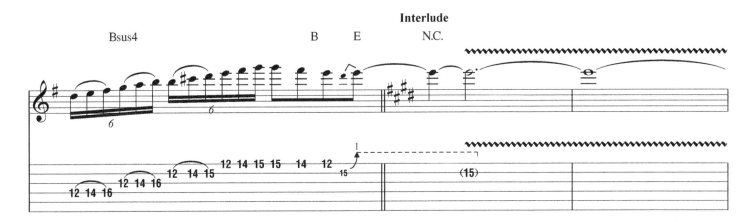

Interlude

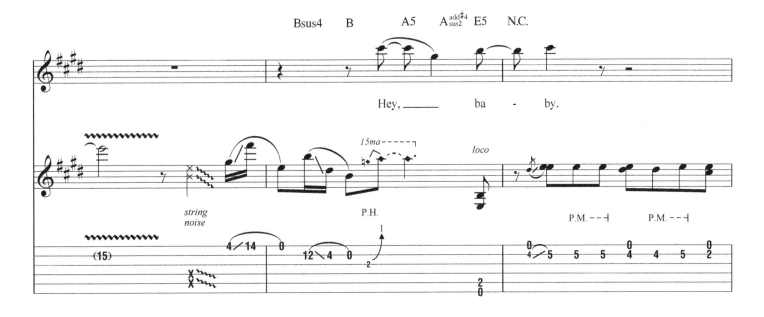

Outro-Chorus

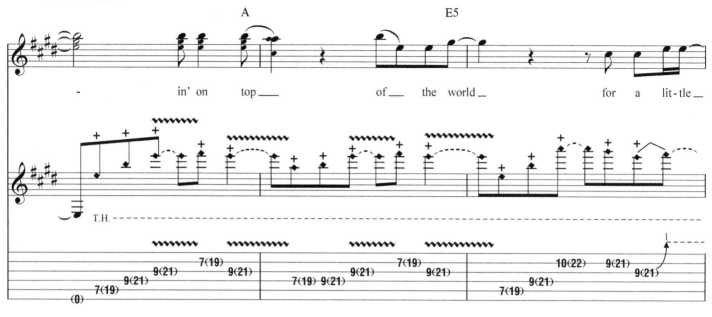

-in' on top ___ of ___ the world ___ for a lit-tle ___

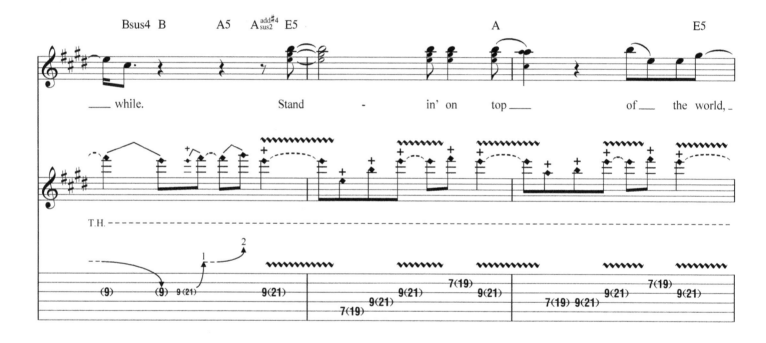

___ while. Stand - in' on top ___ of ___ the world, ___

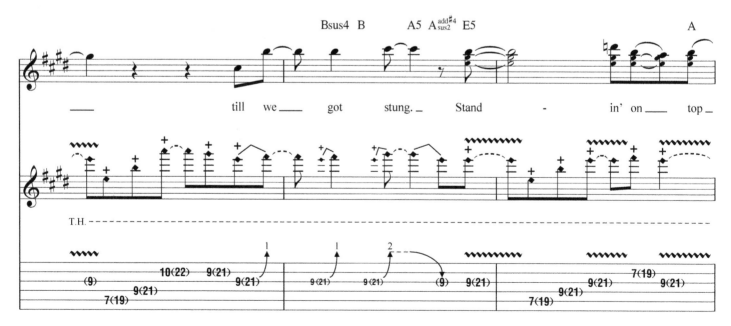

___ till we ___ got stung. ___ Stand - in' on ___ top ___

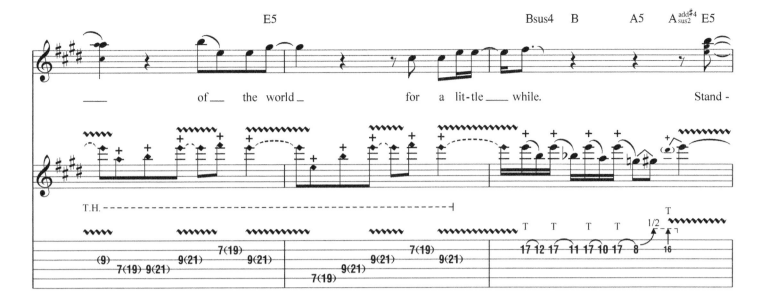

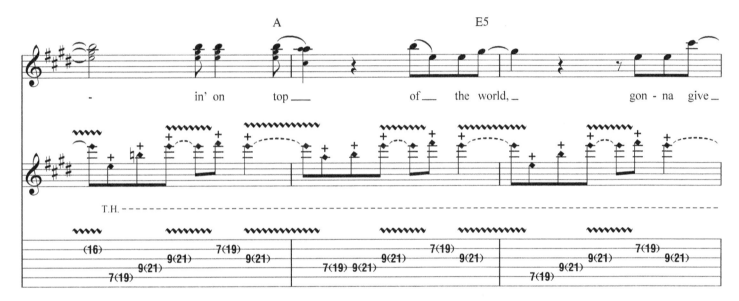

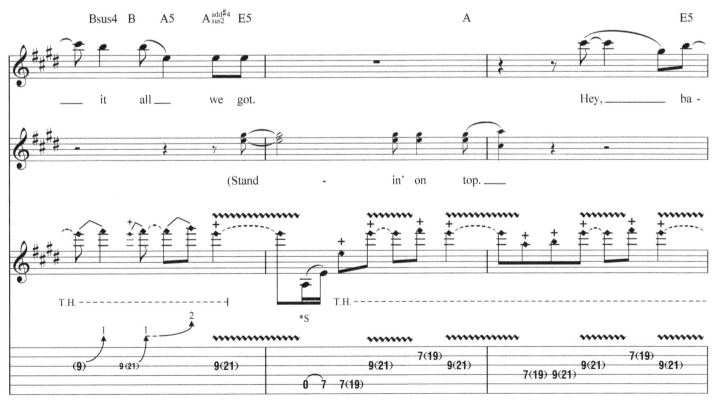

*Slap w/ pick-hand finger.

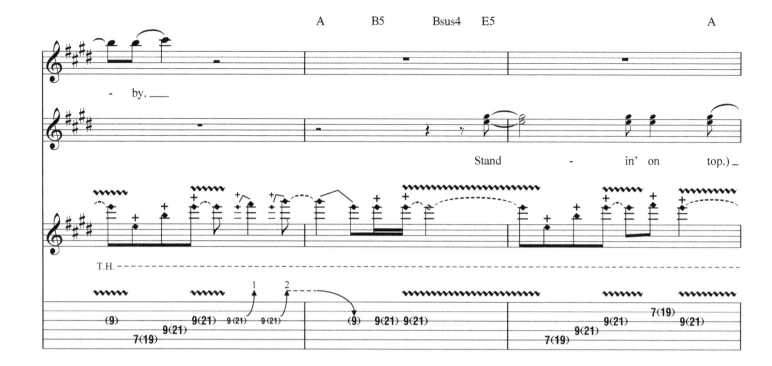

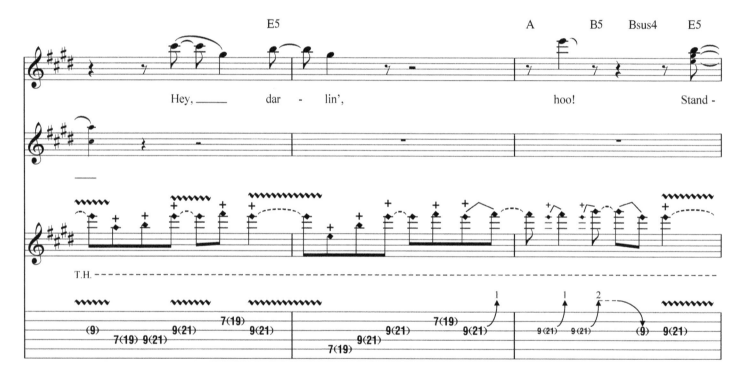

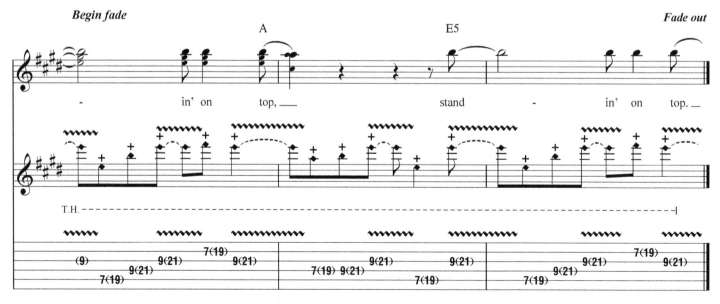

Why Can't This Be Love

Words and Music by Edward Van Halen, Alex Van Halen, Michael Anthony and Sammy Hagar

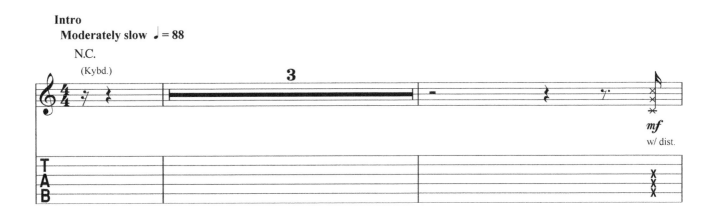

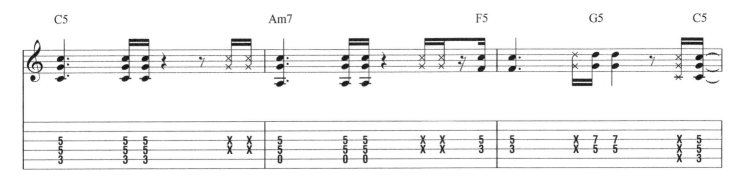

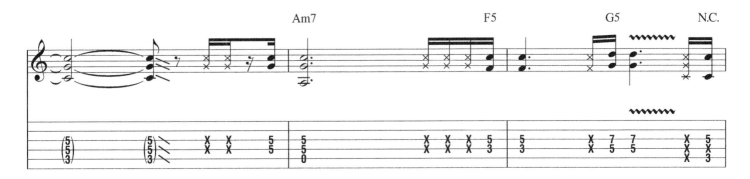

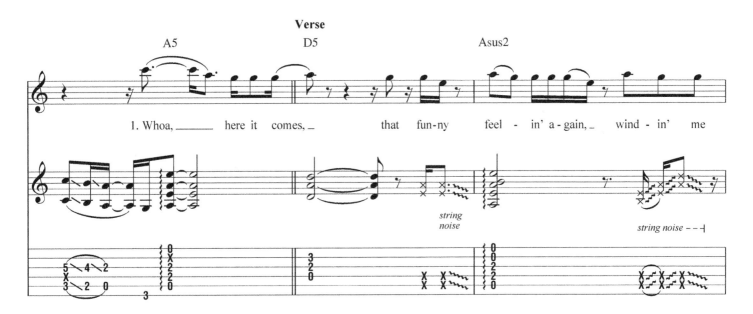

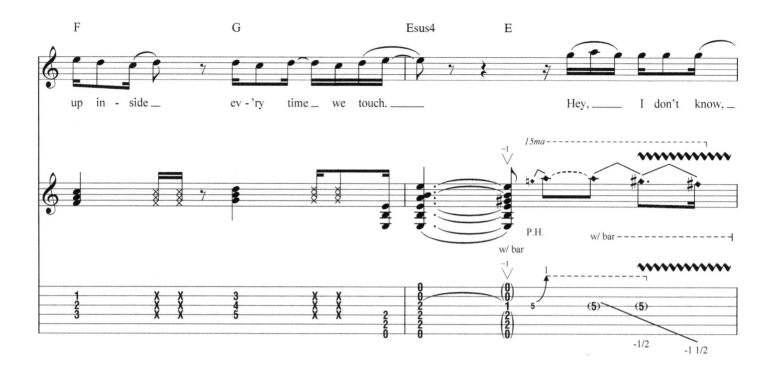

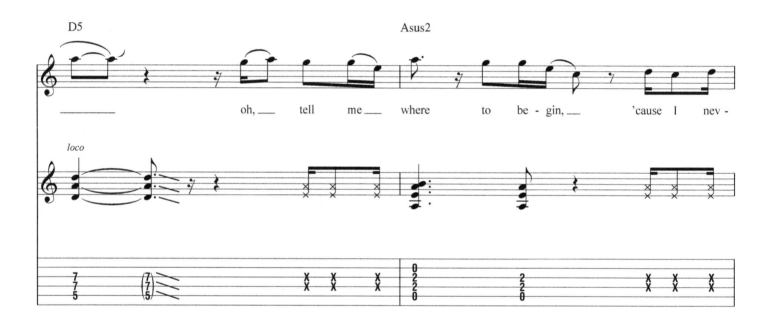

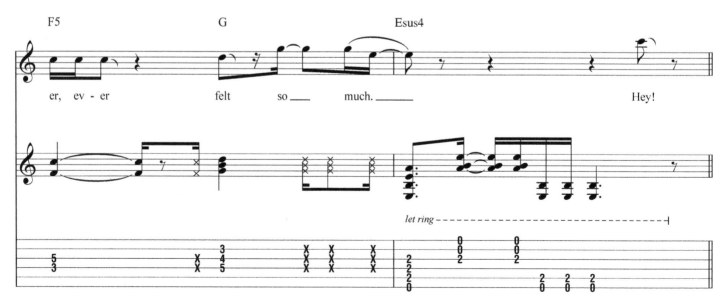

Pre-Chorus

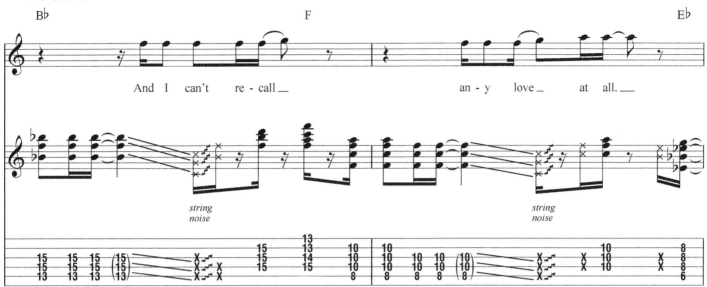

And I can't re-call ___ an - y love ___ at all. ___

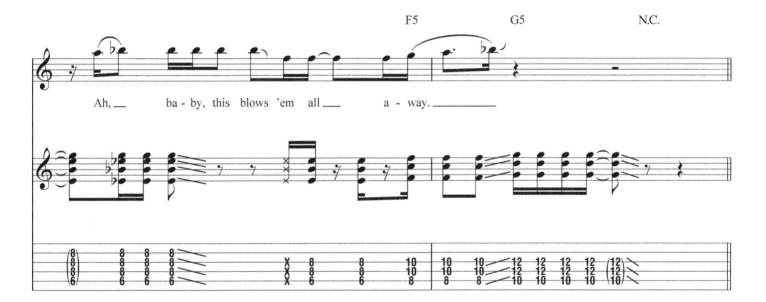

Ah, ___ ba - by, this blows 'em all ___ a - way. ___

Chorus

It's got what it takes, ___ so tell me, why ___

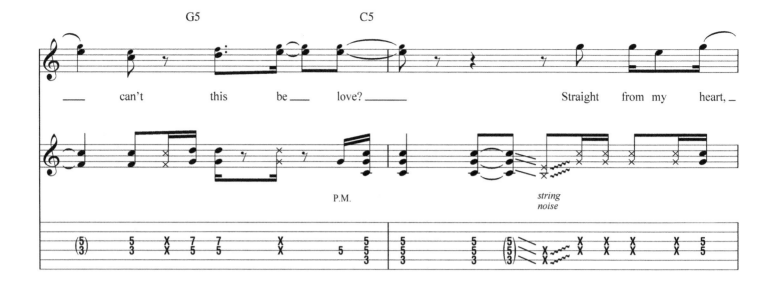

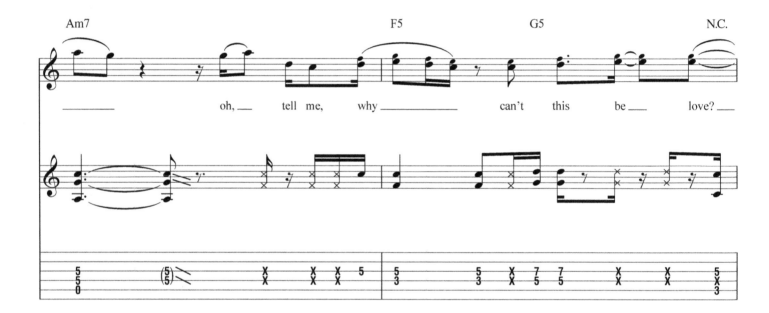

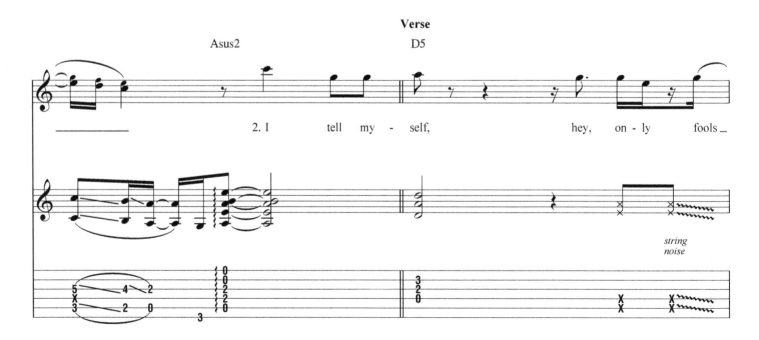

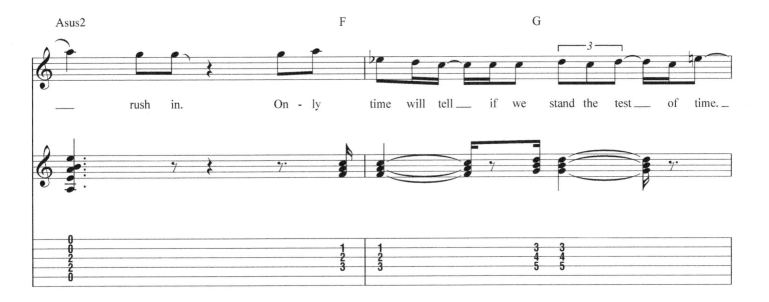

Pre-Chorus

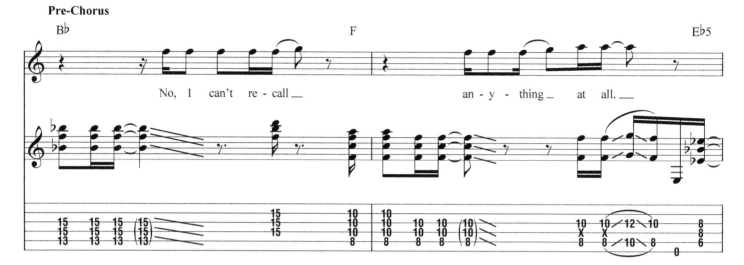

No, I can't re-call __ an-y-thing __ at all. __

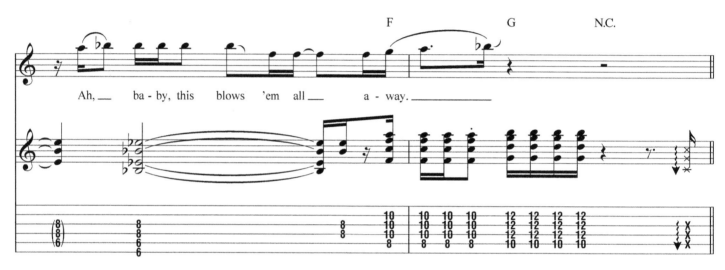

Ah, __ ba-by, this blows 'em all __ a-way. __

Chorus

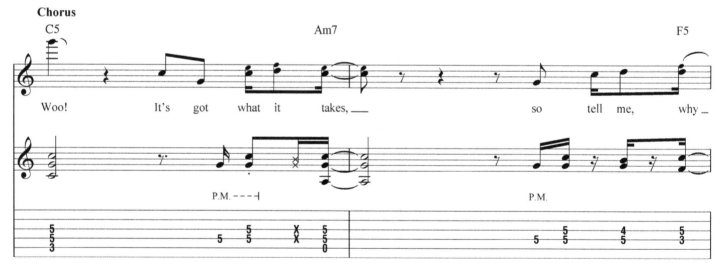

Woo! It's got what it takes, __ so tell me, why __

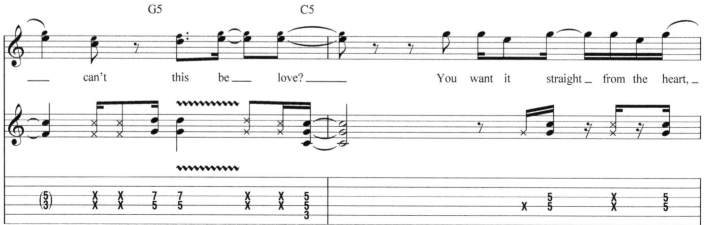

__ can't this be __ love? __ You want it straight __ from the heart, __

oh, _ tell me, why ___ can't this be _ love? ___

Interlude

Da, doo. Da, doo. Da, doo. Da, da, da, doo. Da, doo. Da, doo. Da, _ doo. Da, da, doo.

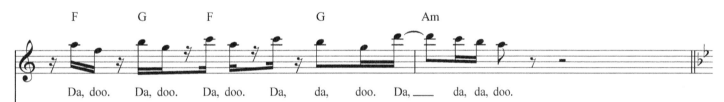

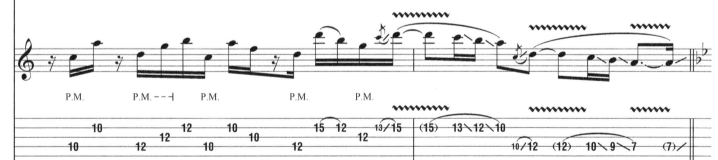

Da, doo. Da, doo. Da, doo. Da, da, doo. Da, ___ da, da, doo.

Guitar Solo

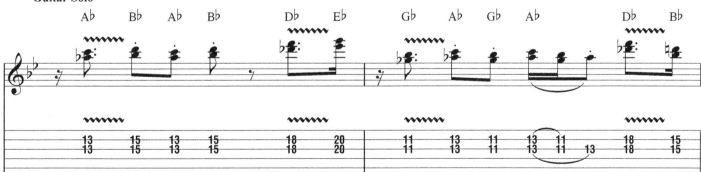

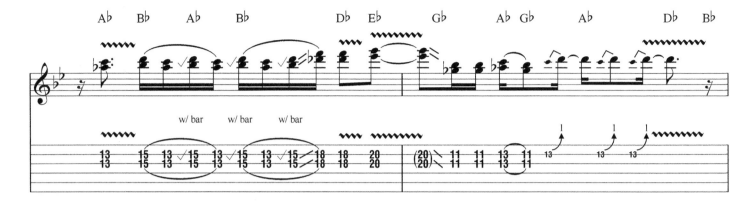

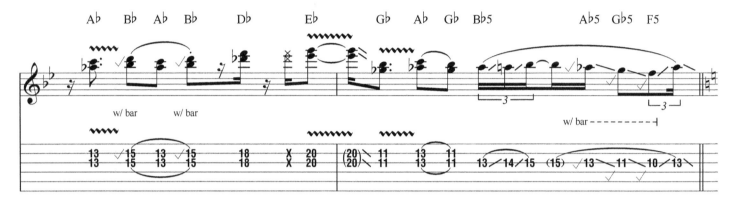

Interlude

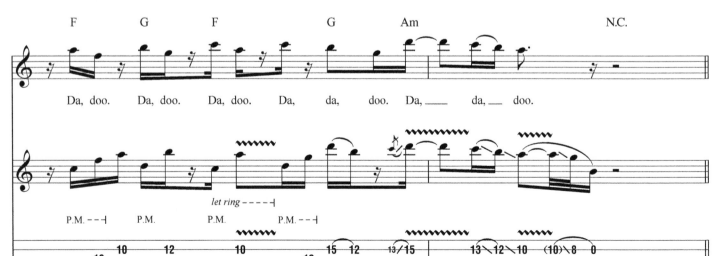

Outro-Chorus

Woo! It's got what it takes, __ so tell me, why __ can't this be __ love? __

__ Straight from the heart, ____ oh, __ tell me, why _____ can't this be __ love? __

_____ Ba-by, why __ can't this be __ love? ____ Got to know, __ why __

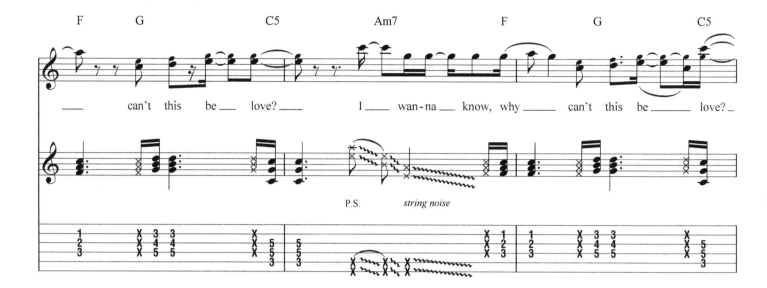

can't this be ___ love? ___ I ___ wan-na ___ know, why ___ can't this be ___ love?

P.S.   *string noise*

Begin fade

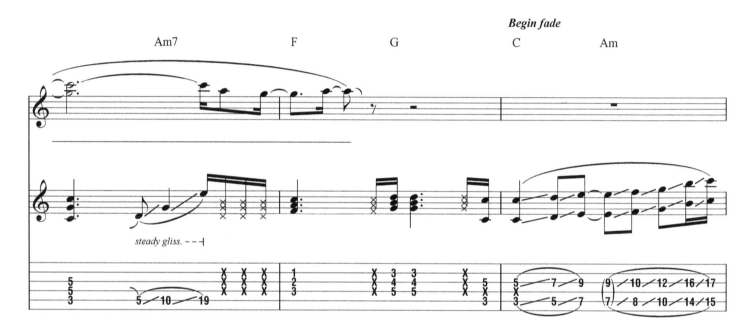

steady gliss. - - -|

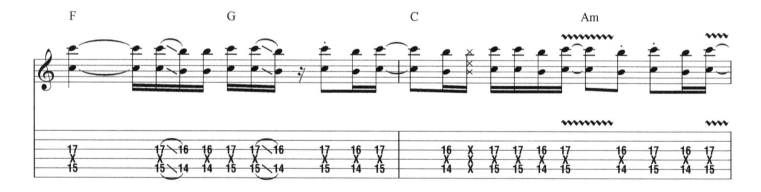

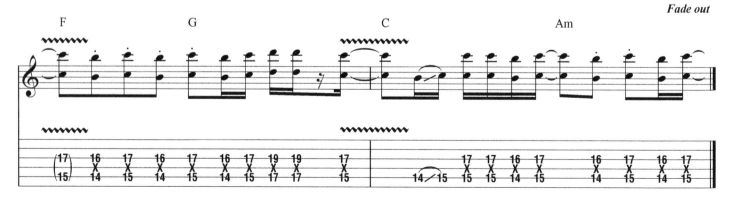

Fade out